C000051342

SETTING HEARTS ON FIRE

A guide to giving evangelistic talks

"Were not our hearts burning within us while he... opened the Scriptures to us?"
LUKE 24:32

---

by John Chapman

MATTHIAS MEDIA

To Phillip Jensen

*Friend, Bible teacher,
evangelist, visionary.*

SETTING HEARTS ON FIRE
1st Edition © John Chapman 1999

St Matthias Press Ltd ACN 067 558 365
PO Box 225, Kingsford, NSW 2032
AUSTRALIA

Ph (02) 9663 1478; Fax (02) 9662 4289
International Ph +61-2-9663 1478; Fax +61-2-9662 4289
E-mail: sales@matthiasmedia.com.au
Internet: http://www.matthiasmedia.com.au

Unless otherwise indicated, Scripture taken from
the HOLY BIBLE, NEW INTERNATIONAL VERSION.
Copyright © 1973, 1978, 1984 International Bible Society.
Used by permission of Zondervan Bible Publishers.

All rights reserved. Except as may be permitted by the Copyright
Act, no portion of this publication may be reproduced in any form
or by any means without prior permission from the publisher.

ISBN 1 876326 15 8

Cover design & typesetting by Joy Lankshear Design Pty Ltd.
Printed in Australia.

Contents

Acknowledgments

Several people helped me to get this book to publication. Adrian Lane of Ridley College in Melbourne read the manuscript and made extensive and helpful comments. The present staff of the Anglican Department of Evangelism in Sydney read the manuscript and discussed it at the Staff retreat in February 1999 and gave me valuable feedback. My particular thanks go to David Mansfield, Steve Abbott, Sheila Spencer, Dominic Steele, and Ruth Muffett and to our Student Ministers Red Fulton, Paul Rees, Marcus Reeves and Orlando Saer. I was glad of their contribution.

Michael Orpwood encouraged me in this project, read manuscripts over and over again, retyped them over and over again, and made helpful comments.

Without these friends it would never have seen the light of day

John C. Chapman
MAY 1999

Introduction

If you are a person who teaches the Bible, whether it is in a Sunday school class, a small group Bible study, Scripture at school, a teenage fellowship group or through preaching sermons, then this book is designed for you. You will, from time to time, want to give a talk that clearly explains to people how they can become a Christian.

Although this book is designed primarily for beginners, I hope it will help us all to rethink what we are doing when we are gospelling, and to be quite clear in our minds about the task. In particular, I will argue that the process of 'preaching the gospel' has both a human and a divine aspect. We are servants of the word of God and we are servants of the people who will be listening to us.

Luke tells us that he gathered information for his gospel from eyewitness who were "servants of the word".[1] They served it by preaching it and preserving it for us. Because of this, we will need to work hard at understanding what the Bible says so that we too can be

---

1.   Lk 1:2

its servants.

The Apostle Paul tells us about his gospelling in these words: "For we do not preach ourselves, but Jesus Christ as Lord, and *ourselves as your servants* for Jesus' sake".[2] He was their slave in bringing the message to them. He preached in such a way that the message was clear, and nothing was put in the way of them knowing about Jesus the Lord.[3]

This is our twin responsibility when we come to give an evangelistic talk: to understand rightly the message of the Bible, and to explain it clearly to our hearers; to be a servant of the word and of the people. Both aspects are vital. Our work will be of no account if it is not the word of God, no matter how clever we are at telling stories or moving people. However, it would be a tragedy if we did understand the message of the Bible but were to obscure it in the way we explained it.

I want to try and address myself to both these issues, in parts 1 and 2 of this book respectively.

I have been doing this work of preaching the gospel for more than forty years. It has brought me more joy than I can express. I hope it helps you to know that joy also.

John C. Chapman
May 1999

---

2. 2 Cor 4:5
3. 1 Cor 1:17; 2 Cor 4:2

PART ONE

Servants of the Word
(LUKE 1:2)

---

*"...they were handed down to us
by those who from the first were eyewitnesses
and servants of the word."*

CHAPTER ONE

What is preaching?

What is in this chapter?
1. There is a word from God to be preached.
2. The words of the Bible are the words of God.
3. Jesus is God's final and complete revelation of God.
4. Preaching is explaining the meaning of the Bible.
5. The Holy Spirit is our helper and so prayer is an essential feature of preaching.

"Preach the Word"
It is hard to imagine a worse situation for any minister of the gospel than that described in 2 Timothy 4:3–4. The apostle Paul is warning Timothy that bad times will come in the church.

> ...men will not put up with sound doctrine. Instead, to suit their own desires, they will gather around them a great number of teachers to say what their itching ears want to hear. They will turn their ears away from the truth and turn aside to myths.

It is a frightening description.

Nothing pleases the gospel minister more than to see

people growing more and more like Christ. And nothing brings more grief than to see the things of God being ignored or people being rebellious to him.

What precedes Paul's description of times to come is a strong exhortation to preach the Word (vv.1–2):

> In the presence of God and of Christ Jesus, who will judge the living and the dead, and in view of his appearing and his kingdom, I give you this charge: Preach the Word; be prepared in season and out of season; correct, rebuke and encourage—with great patience and careful instruction.

In spite of the fact that some will not hear and others will be completely uninterested, Timothy is not to give up. He is to do it when he feels like it and when he doesn't feel like it. It is a serious matter. Timothy is expected to be comprehensive in this speaking role. He is to "correct, rebuke and encourage". Had I been writing this letter I am sure I would have added "with great love", but the Apostle is made of sterner stuff than I am. He is much more practical. He says that it is to be done with "great patience and careful instruction".

I wonder if this method of dealing with such a terrible situation would have been the one that immediately sprang to your mind? I think I probably would have advised Timothy to make it all a matter of prayer, and to call on his friends to do the same. I am sure that he did pray about it. But the real solution was to be found somewhere else. It was to be found in preaching the Word.

A Word to be spoken

The Apostle does not need to explain what he means by this. To say "preach the Word" is sufficient. He is speaking about the word of God, the Spirit-inspired Scriptures that are sufficient for God's person to be equipped for every good work (as they are described in the previous verses).[1] They teach us what to say because they are what God has spoken to his people.

Although God shows us about himself in the creation[2], he most clearly does it by speaking.

> In the past God spoke to our forefathers through the prophets at many times and in various ways, but in these last days he has spoken to us by his Son, whom he appointed heir of all things, and through whom he made the universe.[3]

The God who speaks

For anyone who reads the Bible, this idea is inescapable. Phrases like, "this is what the Lord says", "the word of the Lord came", "God said", and "the law of the Lord" occur frequently throughout its pages. This is so commonplace that the wonder and importance of it can often be overlooked. There are several things to be noted.

1) God speaks to us.

The writer to the Hebrews assumes that his readers will know and agree with him that God has spoken in the past. God did it in many and various way though the prophets. However, God has now done it to us. "In these last days", he tells us, "God has spoken through his Son". You and I are living in "these last days". It was not as if

---

1. 2 Tim 3:16–17
2. Ps 19; Rom 1:18–20
3. Heb 1:1–2

the generations before Jesus were ignorant of God's character or of his promises. But from Jesus onward, everything came into sharper relief. Jesus showed us God's character in his own person and actions.

At the Last Supper, Philip voiced a question that many have asked through the ages. His request was, "Lord, show us the Father and that will be enough for us". He wanted to know what God is really like. Jesus replies:

> Don't you know me, Philip, even after I have been among you such a long time? Anyone who has seen me has seen the Father. How can you say, 'Show us the Father'? Don't you believe that I am in the Father, and that the Father is in me? The words I say to you are not just my own. Rather, it is the Father, living in me, who is doing his work.[4]

Jesus is the last word from God because there is nothing more for God to reveal about himself now that Jesus has come.

2) God speaks to be understood.
It stands to reason that if God speaks to us he expects us to listen to him and to do what he says. He does not speak in such a way that we are in doubt about the message. Jesus is often disappointed when his disciples fail to grasp what he thinks they should know.[5] The parable of the soils warns us of the importance of listening to the teaching of Jesus, as does the parable of the houses built on the rock and the sand. We are expected to hear and obey what God has said.

---

4.   Jn 14:8–10
5.   Lk 24:25; Mk 7:18; Mk 4:40

3) God speaks the truth.

This is so obvious that it hardly needs saying. How would it be possible for God to lie? To say that 'God speaks' implies that there is truth—objective truth—and that God has spoken it. So we are not at all surprised when Jesus says, "I am the way and the truth and the life".[6]

4) God speaks powerfully.

Unlike our words, which are often meaningless and weak, God's words, because they come from God, carry the power to achieve what God wants to do with them.[7] When God decided to create the world, he did it by speaking. God said, "Let there be light" and light there was.[8] We, as preachers, may be weak, but the message of the gospel is not. Indeed, it is the power of God to save people.[9] The same power that made the heavens and the earth is remaking people.[10]

5) God continues to speak to us today from what he said in the past.[11]

In spite of the fact that God has spoken definitively in Christ, he continues to speak to us today from what he has said in the past. His words, which come to us in the pages of the Scriptures, speak to us because we are God's people, and God's method of relating to his people is the same for all ages. When Jesus answers a question put to him about

---

6.   Jn 14:6
7.   Is 55:11
8.   Gen 1:3; Ps 33:6
9.   Rom 1:16
10. 2 Cor 4:6
11. See J. Stott, *I Believe in Preaching* (London: Hodder & Stoughton, 1982) p 100

the nature of the resurrection, he quotes Exodus 3:6 and says to those who ask, "Have you not read *what God said to you*?". If you read Exodus, you will find that God spoke these words to Moses at the burning bush. That they are there in the Scriptures is sufficient for the Lord Jesus to say that God has spoken them to the hearers. They were separated from the event by more than a thousand years, as we are, but such is the nature of God's word that it has eternal significance and relevance for us today. Paul refers to this same idea in his first letter to the Corinthians. He says that the record of the Israelites being punished by God in the wilderness was written for them. Although, once again, it had happened a thousand years before, Paul says, "These things happened to them as examples and were written down as warnings for us, on whom the fulfilment of the ages has come".[12] Since you and I are people on whom the fulfilment of the ages has come, I assume that they have been written for us as well.

6) God speaks to draw us into friendship with him.

It is not insignificant that God speaks to us in so many promises. He not only tells us what he is like, but he draws us into relationship with himself by making promises that he wants us to believe. This trust in the trustworthiness of God's word is the basic Christian experience of God. It is faith that God will do as he has promised.[13] This is spelt out in a wonderful chapter by John Woodhouse in *When God's Voice is Heard* entitled "The Speaker and the Living Word". Commenting on

---

12. 1 Cor 10:11
13. Gen 15:6; Rom 4:21; Rom 10:17

Deuteronomy 4:11–18, he says:

> The nature of true relationship with God is deter-
> mined by the nature of God's revelation. If God
> has approached us by speaking, then to know God
> is to hear and heed his word.[14]

Preaching that Word

When God communicates to his people, he often does it
through human agencies. When he gathered Israel at Mt
Sinai to address them, he did not do that directly but
through Moses, his servant. God regularly addressed his
people through the prophets. He did it supremely and
definitively through the person and word of the Lord
Jesus. He did it through the apostles, and he continues to
do it today through those who teach what the apostles
and the other Bible writers have written.

As the apostle Paul is returning to Jerusalem at the end
of his last missionary journey, he stops at Miletus. From
there he sends to Ephesus and asks the elders of the church
to meet him. This gathering is described in Acts 20. It is the
last time that Paul will see them. In his farewell speech to
them he is anxious that they should understand the nature
of the ministry that has been committed to them. He
knows there will be difficult times ahead: "I know that
after I leave, savage wolves will come in among you and
will not spare the flock. Even from your own number men
will arise and distort the truth in order to draw away disciples after them. So be on your guard!"[15]

---

14. C. Green and D. Jackman (eds), *When God's Voice is Heard*
(IVP, 1994) p 49
15. Acts 20:29-31

Paul reminds them of his own ministry to them. He puts it forward as a model for them to follow. This is how he understands his ministry:

> You know that I have not hesitated to preach anything that would be helpful to you but have taught you publicly and from house to house. I have declared to both Jews and Greeks that they must turn to God in repentance and have faith in our Lord Jesus.[16]
>
> Now I know that none of you among whom I have gone about preaching the kingdom will ever see me again. Therefore, I declare to you today that I am innocent of the blood of all men. For I have not hesitated to proclaim to you the whole will of God.[17]

What he had done was to preach the gospel, the word of God, to them. This is what he wants them to do to each other and to those in that city who are not yet Christians.

Preaching that brings new life

Such preaching is the means God uses to bring us to new birth and to graft us into his family.

> For you have been born again, not of perishable seed, but of imperishable, through the living and enduring word of God. For,
> "All men are like grass, and all their glory is like the flowers of the field;
> the grass withers and the flowers fall,
> but the word of the Lord stands forever."
> And this is the word that was preached to you.[18]

---

16. Acts 20:20-21
17. Acts 20:25-27
18. 1 Pet 1:23-25

The experience of the new birth came to them by the word of God that was preached. In John 3 the new birth is described as a work of the Holy Spirit.[19] It should be noted that the way the Spirit brings us to new birth is inseparably tied up with the preaching of the word of God.

Preaching that brings us to maturity

Paul tells us that the purpose of his preaching and teaching ministry is to bring everyone to maturity.

> We proclaim him (Christ), admonishing and teaching everyone with all wisdom, so that we may present everyone perfect in Christ. To this end I labour, struggling with all his energy which so powerfully works in me.[20]

This same idea is expressed in Ephesians 4:11ff. We are told that the ascended Christ has showered his gifts onto the church.

> It was he who gave some to be apostles, some to be prophets, some to be evangelists, and some to be pastors and teachers, to prepare God's people for works of service, so that the body of Christ may be built up until we all reach unity in the faith and in the knowledge of the Son of God and become mature, attaining to the whole measure of the fullness of Christ.

While it may not be possible to identify each of these 'gifts' with precision, they are all 'word' gifts. The proper exercise of these word gifts is crucial for the church to

---

19. Jn 3:8
20. Col 1:28–29

grow to maturity. The word gifts are fundamental and determinative for all the other gifts in the body of Christ. Whenever preaching and teaching the word of God is neglected, God's people are an easy prey to all sorts of strange teaching.

Elsewhere we are told that the Apostle wants to bring every thought captive to Christ.[21] He urges us to have our minds renewed.[22] It is an awesome responsibility to be a preacher. It is a great privilege, too. When the Bible is handled with care and enthusiasm, people want to self-educate. It inspires them to read the Bible for themselves.

Oliver Barclay, describing the resurgence of biblical and expository preaching among evangelicals in England in the 1950s and 1960s says, "This shifted attention from the speaker to the Bible itself, and encouraged people to study it for themselves".[23]

The mouthpiece of God

In his second letter to the Corinthians, Paul describes himself as the 'ambassador of Christ'. He speaks on Christ's behalf and in that capacity he begs people to be reconciled to God. He tells us that God makes his appeal through him. When Paul exercises the ministry of reconciliation through the message of reconciliation, he is the mouthpiece of God. That is what we are when we too exercise the ministry of reconciliation. We do that by the message of reconciliation. We are the mouthpiece of God.[24]

---

21. 2 Cor 10:5
22. Rom 12:2
23. O. Barclay, *Evangelicalism in Britain 1935-1995* (IVP, 1998) p 135
24. 2 Cor 5:16-21

You may think this to be a grand title for what you are doing. You may be teaching a Scripture class at school, or giving a talk at a teenage fellowship group or at a Bible study group that meets in your home, or you may be a regular preacher in your church, but if you are teaching the word of God properly, then you speak on God's behalf. There is no doubt that the hearers hear the 'voice of God'. That is the wonder of preaching and teaching. A human is speaking but the listeners encounter the living God speaking.

What hinders people from hearing the word of God?

There are at least three ways in which I think people may be hindered from hearing the word of God.

1) Unbiblical teaching.

If what I preach is not, in fact, what the Bible is saying, then it is obvious that the hearers will not hear the word of God. Just because I 'use' the Bible, there is no guarantee that what I am saying is what the Bible is saying. We need to take the greatest care when handling the word of God:

> Do your best to present yourself to God as one approved, a workman who does not need to be ashamed and who correctly handles the word of truth.[25]

The workman who has God's approval is contrasted with the one who does not. The difference between them is the way they handle the word of truth.

---

25. 2 Tim 2:15

2) Showing off.

Instead of being the servant of the Word and a servant of the people, it is possible that the speaker uses the talk to 'show-off'. People remember the speaker but not the message. The message might be correct and orthodox but it is dwarfed by the personality and cleverness of the speaker. I think this is what Paul is referring to when he says:

> For Christ did not send me to baptize, but to preach the gospel—not with words of human wisdom, lest the cross of Christ be emptied of its power.[26]

Paul says this because the Corinthian church had moved into factions. Some were for Paul, some for Apollos, some for Cephas and others for Christ. Paul will have none of it. His preaching was not with worldly wisdom. It was not to draw attention to himself, much less to form a 'party' of followers. No-one ever said, "What a wonderfully clever speaker you are". It was so that the cross of Christ would not be emptied of its power. We need to make this a matter of prayer. There is often a fine line between preaching that is passionate and forceful, in which the issues are put plainly, and preaching that draws attention to the speaker.

3) Spiritual blindness.

Sometimes people do not hear the word of God because they have hardened themselves against the message. This can be described as having 'the eyes of their mind blinded' by the god of this age.[27] Prayer needs to be made that

---

26. 1 Cor 1:17
27. 2 Cor 4:4

God's Holy Spirit will open the mind of the hearers to hear and respond to the word of God.

The preacher—the servant

If what I have said is true, then it should be obvious that preachers must be servants of the word of God. We must work at it to make sure that we understand its message. We are not at liberty to make up something of our own. Preaching is not sharing my thoughts with you but thinking God's thoughts aloud. Our testimonies may be used as an illustration, as might material from church history or current affairs, but they are not the essence of preaching. The essence of preaching is the word of God. We are to listen carefully to what God says to us through his word and then take care to teach it.

In the Anglican service for the ordaining of ministers, the question is asked of the candidate wishing to be ordained, "Will you be diligent in prayer, and in the reading of the Scriptures, undertaking studies that help to a fuller knowledge of them, and turning aside from the pursuit of studies for self-indulgence and worldly gain?"[28] They are expected to answer 'yes' and to take it seriously.

Not only are we to read and study the Bible, but we are to have our lives ordered by it. There should be no difference between what we are saying and the way we are living. I take it that this is the claim of Paul to the Thessalonians:

> You are witnesses, and so is God, of how holy, righteous, and blameless we were among you who believed.[29]

---

28. *An Australian Prayer Book* (1978) p 612
29. 1 Thess 2:10

Not only are preachers the servants of the word. They are to be servants of the people to whom they speak. The following passages are worth pondering:

> For we do not preach ourselves, but Jesus Christ as Lord, and ourselves as your servants for Jesus' sake.[30]
>
> We were gentle among you, like a mother caring for her little children. We loved you so much that we were delighted to share with you not only the gospel of God but our lives as well, because you had become so dear to us.[31]

It is because we are servants of the word that we work hard at understanding the Bible. Because we are servants of the people, we work hard at presenting the message with clarity and passion, showing the relevance and the importance of it to our lives.

The Holy Spirit and the preacher

There is a close relationship between the word of God and the Spirit of God.[32] The Spirit is an active agent in the whole process of preaching and that is why prayer and preaching go together. The Holy Spirit is the author of the Bible and he is its interpreter. He gives us understanding as we study the Scriptures. As preachers, we should approach the whole exercise in an attitude of prayerful dependence on God to help us understand the part of the Bible we are teaching.

The Spirit is also active in the lives of the hearers. It is he who 'shines the light of the gospel' into the hearts and

---

30. 2 Cor 4:5
31. 1 Thess 2:7–8
32. 2 Pet 1:19–21

minds of people.[33] He convinces them of the truth of what they are hearing:

> Our gospel came to you not simply with words, but also with power, with the Holy Spirit and with deep conviction.[34]

The Thessalonians heard the apostle Paul speaking. What he was telling them was the word of God. It was the Spirit who convinced them it was the word of God and so they repented and put their faith in the Lord Jesus.[35] Effective preaching is a supernatural event. We should use the supernatural agency God has given us, namely, prayer. We need to pray that what happened when the apostle Paul preached at Thessalonica will also happen when we preach the word of God.

Prayer and preaching

We should also be at prayer asking God to give us understanding of the word. We should be asking God to give us clarity of mind and of expression so that people will be in no doubt about what God has, in fact, said.[36] We need to pray that the hearer will be enabled to understand and respond positively to what is heard. As well, it is completely desirable to enlist the aid of our friends as we do this.

The seriousness of preaching

Preaching the gospel is an important matter and should be taken seriously by those who do it. I introduced this chap-

---

33. 2 Cor 4:6
34. 1 Thess 1:5
35. 1 Thess 1:9–10
36. Col 4:3–4

ter with the charge that Paul gives to Timothy. Did you notice how seriously Paul takes it?

> In the presence of God and of Christ Jesus, who will judge the living and the dead, and in view of his appearing and his kingdom...[37]

It is a very serious commission whichever way we look at it. His speaking comes under the scrutiny of God and the Lord Jesus. He will give an account of his faithfulness on the Day of Judgement and so will we.

The apostle James has a warning to teachers:

> Not many of you should presume to be teachers, my brothers, because you know that we who teach will be judged more strictly.[38]

Summary

1. There is a Word from God to be preached.
2. When we say accurately what the Bible says we will be the mouthpiece of God.
3. We honour God when we work hard at understanding the Bible.
4. The Holy Spirit is an active agent in both speaker and hearer. Consequently, prayer is essential.

---

37. 2 Tim 4:1
38. Jas 3:1

CHAPTER TWO

What is the gospel we preach?

What is in this chapter

1. The gospel is about Jesus, the Messiah who brings salvation.
2. This is the message of the whole Bible.
3. God created everything well.
4. Sin entered into the creation and ruined it.
5. God's solution to our problem—his King and Servant, Jesus.

Nothing could be more important than that we should be clear about the gospel we are to preach. It is certain that we cannot teach what we do not know. If we are hazy in our minds, it is nearly impossible to speak with any clarity.

What is the gospel?

The message of the gospel can be expressed simply in two words: 'the kingdom'. The Apostle Paul tells the elders from Ephesus, "Now I know that none of you among whom I have gone about preaching the kingdom will ever see me again".[1] He was able to sum up the content of his entire gospel ministry with those two words, and this in one sense reflects the clarity and simplicity of the New Testament gospel. The great announcement of the gospel or 'news' is that Jesus has come as God's Messiah, establishing his kingdom, in which salvation is found through the forgiveness of sins.

I have argued at some length in another place that this is the gospel of Jesus and of Paul and of the New Testament as a whole.[2] It is all about Jesus Christ, the King and Saviour, through whom God reconciles the world to himself.

However, it would be quite wrong to think that this ground-breaking announcement of good news is something completely new, or divorced from the Old Testament. It is in fact the central message of the whole Bible. The message of the Bible is the gospel. It is the story of how God brings his people back into relationship with himself, and keeps them in that relationship, through the work of the Lord Jesus Christ.

When we preach evangelistically, we are really stating the whole message of the Bible in a 'nutshell'. This will have important implications, as we shall see, particularly for the way we read and preach the Old Testament.

First, however, let us get quite clear in our minds what we mean by saying that the gospel is the message of the Bible in a 'nutshell'. What is the message of the Bible? In what sense is it all about Jesus Christ, the Saving Lord?

---

1. Acts 20:25
2 J. Chapman, *Know and Tell the Gospel, 2nd edition* (Matthias Media, 1998) pp 15-40

What is the message of the Bible?

The basic message of the Bible can be summed up in a passage from 2 Corinthians 5:19:

> God was reconciling the world to himself in Christ, not counting men's sins against them.

The story of the Bible is how God achieves this. It has many important themes and sub-themes, the most important of which we will now trace, firstly by looking at the 'shadow' of this reconciling work in the Old Testament, and then at its glorious fulfillment and reality in Jesus.

The Shadow
Creation and Fall

The Bible opens with God creating the world by his word. He speaks it into being. He says, "Let there be light", and so it is.

Humanity is the pinnacle of the creation. This is clear from the way the man 'names' the animals and tends the Garden of Eden in which God has placed him. It is not because he is more intelligent than the animals but because he is qualitatively different, being made in the image of God and having been given dominion by God to rule over the creation under God.[3]

God institutes marriage. Humans are to be social beings as well as spiritual. They are not only related to God and the world around them but they are to relate to one another in a loving and sharing relationship. This is exactly what life was like as it is described for us in the Garden of Eden. We are told that the man and the woman

---

3. Gen 1:26–27

were naked and felt no shame.[4] The symbolism here is beautiful. They were completely exposed. There was nothing they had hidden or wanted to hide from each other. Their deep longings could be shared without fear of laughter or ridicule. There was opportunity for social development and for marriage security.

Provision was made for their spiritual growth. God came and walked with them in the cool of the day and they had fellowship with him. There was a tree in the middle of the garden—a tree called the tree of the knowledge of good and evil. They were not to eat of the fruit of this tree. With the prohibition there was a penalty attached. God said to them:

> "You are free to eat from any tree in the garden; but you must not eat from the tree of the knowledge of good and evil, for when you eat of it you will surely die."[5]

This enabled their spiritual maturity to develop. They had an opportunity to demonstrate to God their love for him by this act of obedience. Without it there was no way to show it. There was food in abundance so that this simple act of obedience was not a burden.

Provision was also made for them to be responsible for the environment. This is the idea behind the 'naming' of the animals and the dominion to be exercised over them as well as the care of the garden.[6]

This wonderful world, as God intended—without fear, hatred or disappointment—is described for us in

---

4.   Gen 2:25
5.   Gen 2:17
6.   Gen 1:26; 2:15

Genesis 1 and 2. It gives a wonderful insight into God's purpose. However it is so foreign to us as to be like fairy-land. By the time we get to the end of the next chapter, we are in a world like ours. There are tensions between the man and the woman. They are no longer friends with God. Work is hard and they are not at one with their environment. We cannot help but ask the question, "What went wrong?".

A reversal of order

In what can only be seen as a reversal of order, we are introduced to an animal— the serpent—who instructs the woman that they should rebel against the God who had been so good to them, and the woman in turn tells the man. They should have been in charge of the animals and not the reverse. The serpent suggests that God has not been good to them at all; that he has, in fact, withheld from them the greatest of all blessings, namely God-hood. He then tempts them with a three-fold rebellion.

The first is to rebel against the word of God. "Did God really say that you were not to eat of any of the trees of the garden?" The woman is quick to correct this misrepresentation. The serpent counters with a suggestion that brings two further rebellions. To her statement that they must not eat or even touch the fruit of the tree of the knowledge of good and evil and that if they do they will die, he says, "That is a lie. God has not given you every good thing. He knows that if you eat it you will become as gods and what's more you will not die." He incites them to rebel against the goodness of God, and also against the idea that God will judge them.

What followed is history. They acted on the three-fold rebellion. They lost their fellowship with God. The punishment of death in the spiritual realm was instantaneous. They were frightened by God's presence. They blamed God for their dilemma. They treated God as their equal. They were spiritually dead. The beginning of the ageing process heralded their physical death. And they were put out of the garden and no longer had access to the tree of life. Nothing could have been worse than for them to live indefinitely in this rebellious state, which is called eternal death. God separated them from the tree of life so that there was a 'breathing time', a time to repent, lest their spiritual death solidify into eternal death.

That was the worst thing that could happen but, in addition, their marriage was under threat. Childbearing was made difficult. The woman was now tempted to dominate the man. The environment was no longer friendly.

There is hope

It is a bleak picture. There is no way for humanity to rectify the situation. They are now 'dead' in their relationship with God. They no longer want God. They are threatened by him. Only an act of God's kindness, or grace, can reverse this situation. Two things assure us that God will intervene. The expulsion from the garden (itself part of the death penalty) gives humanity time and opportunity to repent. This aspect of death has in some sense been delayed. In addition, God gives a promise that the seed of the women will crush the serpent's head. Humanity will triumph over the Evil One.[7]

It may appear that God's plan to make humanity in his own image has been frustrated or even thwarted. This

---

7.   Gen 3:15

is not the case. The rest of the Bible tells the story of how God achieves his plan.

Abraham and the people of God

God calls a man, Abraham, and makes a promise to him, the fulfilment of which will achieve the purposes God had when he created. This promise contains three parts. God will make Abraham's offspring into a great nation—his people. God will give them a land in which to dwell—a second Garden of Eden. And through this people, God will bring blessing to the whole human race.[8]

This three-fold promise began to be fulfilled in the birth of Abraham's son, Isaac, through Isaac's son, Jacob, and through Jacob's twelve sons. By various circumstances, Jacob and his twelve sons came into Egypt, where they did, in fact, grow into a great nation just as God had promised. But, as yet, they did not have their own land. They were slaves in the land of Egypt.

God, true to his promise, saved them from their slavery. He raised up Moses to lead them to their Promised Land. This rescue—or exodus—God achieved for them. They were powerless to achieve it for themselves. He intervened and redeemed them. He brought them to Mt Sinai where he gave them the law so they could give full expression to their love and thankfulness to him through their obedience.[9]

Because they were a people on the move, and because they lived in tents, God instructed them to make a tent for him. It was called 'the tabernacle'. It represented God's

---

8.   Gen 12:2–3
9.   You can read this in Gen 15–50 and Ex 1–40.

presence with his people. It was carried in front of them when they were on the move, and when they camped it was pitched in the middle of the encampment. Its symbolism was obvious. This continued until the tabernacle was replaced under the reign of King Solomon who built the temple at Jerusalem. This permanent building on a permanent site was to show that God would always be with his people.[10]

As well as the law, God gave his people a system of sacrifices. Some were designed to show them that, when they had sinned, something needed to be done for them to be restored into fellowship with God again. Others were designed to keep their relationship with God healthy.

The people of God were delayed from entering into the Promised Land because of their disobedience to God. The delay lasted until an entire generation had died out. This forty-year wilderness wandering is described in the book of Numbers. It is a sorry time in their history. The purposes of God seem to dim and almost to disappear.

However, a new generation under a new leader entered the Promised Land and took possession of it at God's command. Once again God gave them victories over their enemies which they would not have achieved without him. It was grace again![11] However they failed to achieve what God required of them. They did not drive out all the nations as they were bidden, and their continued disobedience should have disqualified them from being God's people.

True enough, they were God's people, but they did

---

10. See 1 Kgs 6–9.
11. See the book of Joshua.

not live as if they were. They were in their land, but not all of it, and they were not a blessing to the whole human race. They were meant to be an object lesson to all the nations of the world. They were to show how wonderful it was for a nation to have God as their God. Instead they behaved like every other nation around them.

Although God was their king and protector, they asked God to give them a king like the nations around them, to rule them and bring peace and justice, and to drive out their enemies. It was a rejection of God but he graciously allowed them to have such a king to do as they had requested.[12]

A King for God's people

Under the reigns of Kings David and Solomon, the hopes of the people of God for their king were almost achieved. Those kings did save Israel from its enemies. They did rule with justice. Those kings respected God's rule and sought to live under it. They enlarged the borders of Israel and the people became very prosperous. Solomon built the temple and God graced it with his presence. The visit of the Queen of Sheba to the court of Solomon was like the beginning of the fulfilment of the promise that all the nations would be blessed through God's people.[13] However, as great as those two kings were, their feet were of clay. They sinned and they lead Israel to sin. Their successors were a pitiful lot who, with rare exceptions, lead Israel into idolatry. They did not give justice to the poor but ground them into the earth. They behaved like the nations around them. They

---

12. See 1 Sam 8–9.
13. 1 Kgs 10

were not distinctively God's.

They gave up on God, but mercifully he did not give up on them. Over a period of hundreds of years, God sent the prophets to his people to call them back to himself.

Promises of renewal—a King and a Servant

Not only did God call his people back to repentance, he also made new promises that he would change them so they would want to obey him instead of always disobeying him. This is one from Jeremiah:

> "The time is coming", declares the Lord, "when I will make a new covenant with the house of Israel and with the house of Judah... I will put my law in their minds and write it on their hearts. I will be their God, and they will be my people. No longer will a man teach his neighbour or a man his brother, saying, 'Know the Lord', because they will all know me, from the least of them to the greatest", declares the Lord. "For I will forgive their wickedness and will remember their sins no more."[14]

A similar one comes from the prophet Ezekiel:

> "I will cleanse you from all your impurities and from all your idols. I will give you a new heart and put a new spirit in you; I will remove from you your heart of stone and give you a heart of flesh. And I will put my Spirit in you and move you to follow my decrees and be careful to keep my laws."[15]

In addition to these promises was another cluster of promises about a new king, a king like David and

---

14. Jer 31:31; 33–34
15. Ezek 36:25–27

Solomon, but without their flaws. This king, or Messiah, would not only drive out their enemies and cause them to live properly with each other and with God but he would be the means of bringing them back into the 'new' promised land, the 'new' Eden.[16] This kingdom would be an everlasting kingdom. It would be the fulfilment of all God's promises.[17]

As well as this King, the prophet Isaiah told of the Servant of God who would take upon himself the sins of God's people and be the means of their total forgiveness.[18]

The Reality
The Kingdom is near.

Hundreds of years went by. The fulfilment of God's promises seemed as far away as ever. Yet, in a godly remnant, the hope for their Messiah King was kept alive. John the Baptist's arrival on the scene electrified the people of God with the announcement that the kingdom of God was near. The long-promised king was near at hand. They should ready themselves by repenting or else be swept away by him in judgement.[19] The Lord Jesus comes with the same message.[20]

Jesus is the fulfilment of all God's promises and purposes.

There is no doubt that, as we read the Gospels and the rest of the New Testament, Jesus is the fulfiller of all of God's promises. In fact, the whole of the Old Testament is

---

16. Is 11; Ps 2
17. Dan 7:13–14
18. Is 52:13–53:12
19. Matt 3:1–12
20. Mk 1:15

really about him.[21] God has been preparing us through everything that went before so that we would recognise Jesus in all his fullness. Although the events already described were real themselves, they were a 'shadow' of The Reality, which is Christ.

Jesus and Adam.

When God created humanity, it was in "his own image".[22] The entry of sin marred this image. No longer was it possible to see God's character by looking at the man or the woman, or at any other men or women. We had to wait until Jesus came before we saw again a human in the image of God.[23] To know Jesus was to know the Father.[24] Unlike Adam and Eve, Jesus would not heed the Evil One when he tempted him to disobedience. Adam and Eve were surrounded by every evidence of God's goodness and failed. Jesus was tested in the desert[25] and suffered on the cross[26], yet he continued to obey his Father. When God said, "Let us make man in our own image" it was with the Lord Jesus in view. Jesus fulfilled the purposes of God. Yet it does not stop there. We, who are in Christ, are having the image of God restored in us.[27] It will be done perfectly when Jesus returns and takes us to be with him in the new creation.[28] God's purposes are not thwarted.

---

21. Jn 5:39–40
22. Gen 1:26
23. 2 Cor 4:4
24. Jn 14:9–10
25. Matt 4:1–11
26. Matt 27:41–43
27. 2 Cor 3:18; Rom 8:29
28. 1 Jn 3:2

Jesus—the seed of the woman.

The promise given to Adam and Eve at the time of the Fall, that the seed of the woman would crush the head of the serpent, was fulfilled in the Lord Jesus. No doubt when Eve gave birth to Cain, her first born, she thought he would be the 'head-crusher'. She was sorely mistaken. Jesus defeated the power of Satan when he died on the cross. He took the punishment our sins deserved. He opened a way for our total forgiveness, thus snatching us from the power of the Evil One.[29] As before, we who are in Christ, will have Satan crushed under our feet.[30]

Jesus—the promise to Abraham—and the people of God.

When God made his promise to Abraham that he would give him a people and that all the nations of the world would be blessed through them, it was really Jesus he was speaking about.[31] Jesus is the true 'people of God'. Israel is referred to as the vine in Isaiah 5, but Jesus says that *he is the true vine* in John 15 and that, by union with him, we are the true people of God. This is just one of many similar examples of how references to Israel are applied to the Lord Jesus. Unlike Israel, who failed again and again in their wilderness wandering, Jesus the true Israelite did not fail in his temptations.[32]

Jesus is the light to the Gentiles. It is through him that the world mission is to take place. The gospel is for all nations. In Jesus, all the nations of the world will indeed be blessed.[33]

---

29. Col 2:13–15; Lk 11:14–22
30. Rom 16:20
31. Gal 3:16
32. Matt 4:1–11
33. Matt 28:28

Jesus and the Exodus.

Moses is used by God to save his people from their slavery and to bring them to their Promised Land. This is a picture of the great Exodus, which Jesus performs through his death and resurrection. By his sin-bearing sacrifice, he sets the captives free from sin and death. He sets us free to serve God and he will bring us to the new creation, which he is preparing.[34] On the mountain when the Lord Jesus was transfigured, Moses and Elijah came and spoke with Jesus about the 'exodus' which he would fulfil in Jerusalem.[35] The exodus that Moses achieved was a pale shadow of the great exodus that Jesus achieved.

Jesus and the sacrificial system.

The sacrificial system that God gave to his people at Mt Sinai was really a picture of the Lord Jesus. He was the Lamb of God, who bore the sin of the world.[36] When Jesus took our punishment in his death on the cross, he brought permanent forgiveness for us. He was perfect and without sin. He needed no forgiveness. We, on the other hand, are sinful and under the punishment of death.[37] Jesus took that punishment when he died for us and for the sins of the whole world.[38] He opened a permanent way back to God. His sacrifice was better than that of any previous sacrifice because it was permanent, as the letter to the Hebrews argues.[39] When we look at the death of Jesus for us, we

---

34. Col 2:13–15; Jn 14:1–4; Rev 21–22
35. Lk 9:31
36. Jn 1:29
37. Rom 6:23
38. 1 Jn 2:1–2
39. Heb 9–10

know that God loves us. We know that sin matters and will not go unpunished. We know, also, that God is merciful. We experience all these attributes of God, in perfect harmony.

Jesus—the Tabernacle and the Temple.

When Jesus said, "Destroy this temple, and I will raise it again in three days"[40] he was talking about his bodily resurrection from the dead. His disciples recognised this after the event.[41] It is Jesus who is the temple of God. We meet the Father through the Son. He is God in the midst of his people and he is the place where God dwells. We, too, as individual Christians and as the church, are the temple of God when we are 'in Christ'.[42]

Jesus—the King and the Suffering Servant.

Supremely, Jesus fulfils all the promises about the Messiah who would come, and the Suffering Servant. The voice of God, which was heard at Jesus' baptism and at the Mount of Transfiguration, said, "You are my beloved Son in whom I am well pleased". Those who knew their Old Testament would have recognised that these were two quotations. One was from Psalm 2 and the other from Isaiah 42. One refers to the Messiah, the King of Israel, and the other to the Suffering Servant.

Jesus explained this to his disciples. They had confessed that he was the Messiah, and he began to teach them that he would suffer, die and be raised to life again.[43]

---

40. Jn 2:19
41. Jn 2:19–22
42. 1 Cor 6:19; 3:16
43. Matt 16:16–23

The sayings and miracles of Jesus showed the extent of his kingly rule. He showed himself to be Lord over the bodies and minds of people. He healed the sick, he forgave sins, and he raised the dead. There was no aspect of life in the creation over which he was not Lord. He exorcised demons. Even they were subject to him.

Until Jesus came, no one had ever thought that the King could also be the Suffering Servant. They seemed to be mutually exclusive. Many of Jesus' contemporaries had been brought up all their life to think of Messiah in terms of Psalm 2, where God says to his King:

> ...You are my Son;
> today I have become your Father.
> Ask of me, and I will make the nations your inheritance,
> the ends of the earth your possession.
> You will rule them with an iron sceptre;
> you will dash them to pieces like pottery,[44]

It seemed an impossibility that Jesus should:

> suffer many things and be rejected by the elders and teachers of the law and that he must be killed and after three days rise again.[45]

to say nothing of the fact that he would be:

> handed over to the Gentiles. They will mock him, insult him, spit on him, flog him and kill him. On the third day he will rise again.[46]

Yet this is exactly what he did.

---

44. Ps 2:7–9
45. Mk 8:31
46. Lk 18:31–33

He taught the disciples that true greatness was through humble service. He said, "The Son of Man did not come to be served, but to serve, and to give his life as a ransom for many".[47] Not only was he Messiah and Suffering Servant, he was also the Son of Man (from Daniel 7).

There was no doubt that Jesus was the King. His resurrection from the dead was irrefutable evidence of this. The disciples saw it to be a direct fulfilment of the promise "you will not abandon me to the grave nor will you let your Holy One see decay".[48] So they boldly proclaimed, "God has made this Jesus, whom you crucified, both Lord and Christ".[49] In this capacity he has been appointed the judge of the living and the dead.[50] That is why repentance is a proper response to him.

Judgement is a major theme of the gospel. In Revelation 14:6, an angel has an 'eternal' gospel to proclaim to those who dwell on earth. Does this mean a gospel for the age to come or a gospel that will last forever? Whatever it means, please note its content. The angel cries out:

> Fear God and give him glory, because the hour of
> his judgement has come. Worship him who made
> the heavens, the earth, the sea, and the springs of
> water.[51]

There was no doubt that Jesus was the Suffering Servant. The apostle Peter described him in this way—"He himself

---

47. Mk 10:45
48. Ps 16:10
49. Acts 2:36
50. Jn 5:19–30
51. Rev 14:7

bore our sin in his body on the tree."[52] Another writer says of him, "God made him who had no sin to be sin for us, so that in him we might become the righteousness of God."[53]

Jesus—the centre of all God's purposes.

It is clear that there is no way we can come to God except through the person and work of the Lord Jesus. We may not come to the Father except through the Son and we will not experience the Holy Spirit except through the Son. Jesus is at the centre of all God's plans. All the promises of God reach their fulfilment in him:

> For no matter how many promises God has made, they are "Yes" in Christ. And so through him the 'Amen' is spoken by us to the glory of God. [54]

If it can be said with reverence, the Lord Jesus was in the 'back of God's mind' when God said at the beginning, "Let there be light". This is how the apostle Paul describes the Lord Jesus:

> He is the image of the invisible God, the firstborn over all creation. For by him all things were created: things in heaven and on earth, visible and invisible, whether thrones or powers or rulers or authorities; all things were created **by him and for him...so that in everything he might have the supremacy.**[55]

The kingdom has arrived in Jesus, but it is not yet

---

52. 1 Pet 2:24
53. 2 Cor 5:21
54. 2 Cor 1:20
55. Col 1:15–18

completed. We still wait for the Lord Jesus to return from heaven and to usher in the New Creation where all those who are Christ's, from all the nations, will be the people of God, with him in the 'land' which God had promised to Abraham.

While the Bible taken as a whole is the message of the gospel, there are summaries of it available to us. When the Philippian jailer asks the apostle Paul, "What must I do to be saved?" the answer is given, "Believe in the Lord Jesus, and you will be saved".[56] The whole 'box and dice' can be summed up in one sentence. God has summarised or fulfilled it in Jesus. Without Jesus there is no gospel.

The Apostle Paul says:

> I want to remind you of the gospel I preached to you, which you received and on which you have taken your stand. By this gospel you were saved, if you hold firmly to the word I preached to you... For what I received I passed on to you as of first importance: that Christ died for our sins according to the Scriptures, that he was buried, and that he was raised on the third day according to the Scriptures.[57]

This is another summary.

However, when we preach these summaries, which we will, care needs to be taken not to make the part sound different from the whole. We need to keep the overall picture in the back of our minds. This should prevent us from making foolish statements when dealing with the summaries.

Let me clarify what I am saying and what I am not. It

---

56. Acts 16:30–33
57. 1 Cor 15:1–3

is possible to expound some part of the Bible while not setting it in the wider message of the Bible as a whole. In such a case, it will not be the gospel. It would be possible to expound a passage like Matthew 7:13-14 and urge people to enter through the narrow gate and choose life. However, if the sermon does not focus on Christ, it is not the gospel, even though it comes from the Bible.[58]

I have heard evangelistic sermons preached where the saving work of Jesus was so emphasised that it dwarfed his kingly rule and we were led to believe that if we put our trust in Jesus for salvation all would be well. The part was made to sound different from the whole. This could be done in the opposite direction by so stressing the Lordship of Jesus that faith disappeared from our response and was subsumed by repentance.

It is a great gospel to preach and God uses it to call people back to himself.

Summary

1. All of God's purposes for the creation are fulfilled in his Son, Jesus Christ.
2. God's gospel is about Jesus.
3. Jesus is true Israel, God's King, the Suffering Servant and the Judge of all the world.
4. In as much as we are 'in Christ', we too fulfil the purposes of God for us.

---

58. Rom 1:3

CHAPTER THREE

What is evangelistic preaching?

What is in this chapter?

1. All preaching is evangelistic preaching when it is set in its biblical context, because it points to Jesus.
2. Specific evangelistic preaching can be recognised by these features:
    (a) its content is a summary of the whole Bible message of Jesus as the Saving Messiah;
    (b) it is aimed specifically at unbelievers;
    (c) its style is controlled by the target audience (eg. absence of jargon and technical terms, user-friendly).

If you are a regular teacher of the Bible, there is a very good chance that you have already engaged in evangelistic preaching, whether you knew it or not. But just in case you haven't, we should be clear about what it is we are doing when we preach the gospel.

We have already seen that the message of the Bible is about how God rescues rebellious humanity through the person and work of Jesus. There are lots of things about God that we do not know even when we have read the Bible; but what we do know is how to get right with God.

The Bible is about God and our salvation. It is about how God reconciles the world to himself in Christ.

This is how the apostle Paul describes the Scriptures:

> ...from infancy you have known the holy Scriptures, which are able to make you wise for salvation through faith in Christ Jesus. All Scripture is God-breathed and is useful for teaching, rebuking, correcting and training in righteousness, so that the man of God may be thoroughly equipped for every good work.[1]

These Scriptures of which Paul is speaking are the Old Testament Scriptures, which Timothy's mother and his grandmother had taught him from infancy. These Scriptures are able to make him "wise for salvation". If he understands the message they contain and takes appropriate action, he will be saved. He will be a true Christian. That is because the Old Testament Scriptures are about God and salvation. However, they are incomplete on their own. They will make us wise for salvation *through faith in Christ Jesus*. The Lord Jesus is the interpreter of the Old Testament Scriptures. Without him they are incomplete. He is the key to understanding them, because he is the key to salvation.

This idea was one that the Lord Jesus held. In a part of John's Gospel where Jesus is arguing with the Pharisees, he explains it this way:

> For the very work that the Father has given me to finish, and which I am doing, testifies that the Father has sent me. And the Father who sent me has himself testified concerning me. You have never

---

1.   2 Tim 3:15–16

heard his voice nor seen his form, nor does the word dwell in you, for you do not believe the one he sent. You diligently study the Scriptures because you think that by them you possess eternal life. These are the Scriptures that testify about me, yet you refuse to come to me to have life... But do not think that I will accuse you before the Father. Your accuser is Moses, on whom your hopes are set. If you believed Moses, you would believe me, for he wrote about me. But since you do not believe what he wrote, how are you going to believe what I say?[2]

The terrible tragedy is that, while they studied the Bible diligently, they had failed to understand its meaning. It was all pointing to Jesus. Jesus must have been referring to the Old Testament Scriptures since none of the New Testament was written at that time. The whole of the Old Testament is about the Lord Jesus, and he is the key to understanding it. While it is the word of God, if we fail to see its connection with Jesus, we will not grasp its true meaning. Under the Holy Spirit, the Old Testament writers were telling us about the Mighty King who would come and rescue God's people.

If you have been teaching the Bible properly, you will have been teaching the gospel, for the Bible's overall message is about Jesus, and Jesus is the gospel.

Jesus—the key

Luke expresses the same idea when he describes the two persons who meet Jesus as they are walking from Jerusalem to Emmaus. This was the day that Jesus rose from the dead,

---

2. Jn 5:36–40, 45–47

but they did not know this fact. They were disappointed and disillusioned because they had thought that Jesus was the Messiah.

Jesus joined them on the road, but they were kept from recognising him. In answer to his question, they tell Jesus what they thought about him.

> "He was a prophet, powerful in word and deed before God and all the people. The chief priests and our rulers handed him over to be sentenced to death, and they crucified him; but we had hoped that he was the one who was going to redeem Israel. And what is more, it is the third day since all this took place. In addition, some of the women amazed us. They went to the tomb early this morning but didn't find his body. They came and told us that they had seen a vision of angels, who said he was alive. Then some of our companions went to the tomb and found it just as the women had said, but him they did not see."
>
> He said to them, "How foolish you are, and how slow of heart to believe all that the prophets have spoken! Did not the Christ have to suffer these things and then enter his glory?" And beginning with Moses and all the Prophets, he explained to them what was said in all the Scriptures concerning himself.[3]

Here again we see that failure to understand the Old Testament is failure to recognise Jesus. They should not have been taken by surprise by the events in Jesus' life. These were foretold in the Old Testament sSriptures.

Later that same day, Jesus appeared to a group of his

---

3. Lk 24:19–27

friends in the upper room. He reminded them yet again of this truth.

> "This is what I told you while I was still with you: Everything must be fulfilled that is written about me in the Law of Moses, the Prophets and the Psalms."
>
> Then he opened their minds so they could understand the Scriptures. He told them, "This is what is written: The Christ will suffer and rise from the dead on the third day, and repentance and forgiveness of sins will be preached in his name to all nations..." [4]

It was to all of the three sections of the Old Testament that Jesus made his appeal—the Law (i.e. the Torah, the first five books), the Prophets (which included the history of Joshua through to Kings, as well as the writing prophets) and the Wisdom literature (the Psalms, Proverbs and the like). All of it was pointing to Jesus. It is through him that it is all to be understood.

We can be sure that if we have been teaching the Old Testament and a Jew is happy with our explanation, it cannot be Christian. Overarching everything is Jesus and salvation.

Every talk evangelistic

There is a sense, then, in which every talk will be evangelistic. When it is shown how the particular part of the Bible being taught is related to the whole, then it will be related to Christ and salvation.

If you are doing a series on Leviticus and cannot show how this relates to Jesus and salvation, you probably do

---

4. Lk 24:44–47

not know what Leviticus is about. It all fits into the pattern somehow, and our job as teachers is to show how.

It is worth noting what I am not saying. I am not saying that at the end of every talk we tack on John 3:16 and urge people to 'turn to Christ', whether this has any bearing on what we have been talking about. I heard a talk like that once. It had been advertised as "Advance Australia Where?". It was at the time when the Australian government decided to change the national anthem from 'God Save the Queen' to 'Advance Australia Fair'. I thought it was such a clever title and that I would hear a talk about national apostasy. So I went. The talk began with a tirade against the government for changing the old anthem (which was a prayer) to the new anthem (which was a song of national pride). We were assured that this 'song' would never be sung in that church. However, to my astonishment, the speaker, having told us this, continued by saying "and here are five reasons why you can be sure that Jesus rose from the dead". I could hardly believe my ears! The first part of the talk seemed to have nothing to do with the second part.

When I say that each part is to be related to the whole, I am not talking about a massive 'gear' change but the logical outcome of carefully showing how this particular part takes its place in the overall revelation that God has made.

The context is important

Every competent teacher of the Bible knows how important it is to 'set' the particular verse or story into its context. When this is not done, it is possible to change and distort the meaning of the Bible.

A friend of mine chooses a verse of the Bible to be his 'motto' for the year. I saw him one New Year's Day and asked him what his verse for that year was. With a glint in his eye, he said, "Woe unto them who rise up early in the morning".

"Where does it come from?" I asked.

"Isaiah 5:11", was the reply.

When I looked it up and read it in its context I realised that I'd been had! Its meaning had been considerably changed. It wasn't about getting up early or sleeping at all.

I have heard several talks on Revelation 3:20 as if it was addressed to unbelievers and not the church, and as if the person knocking at the door was not the mighty and impressive person who has been described for us in Revelation 1:12–17. This passage is directed to a church that was on the brink of extinction. It only needed one, just one, to 'hear his voice' and he would again fellowship with them as he had in the past. Had the context been taken into consideration, we would never have been told in the talk the nonsense that the Lord God is incapable of opening the door unless we let him. I ask you!

It is important to get the context of a particular passage of the Bible right, both what has preceded it and what follows it. We need to ask why the writer has set it in this place and not in another.

The part in the particular book

As well as thinking about the immediate context, we need to see how the particular part we are working on fits into the whole book of the Bible from which the part comes. It is important that, when we have taught on a particular passage, what we say should 'sound' like the rest of that book. I often hear students preaching their first evangelistic talks. When they want to convince us that we are sinners they will, almost without exception, take us to Romans 3:23 and remind us that "all have sinned and fall short of the glory of God". I would be delighted if the passage they were expounding came from Romans. However it seems not to have occurred to them that, if the passage came from John, there might be a Johannine way of convincing us that we were sinners. I would give John 3:19–21 a try instead. I agree that it requires much more work, but it allows us to say the same ideas over and over again without saying the same words. This enables us to teach the same truths without being predictable and boring, and to treat the work with integrity.

It is important to know that some authors do not use terms that are common to other authors and that some words have slightly different meanings from one author to another. John's gospel does not have the word 'repentance' in it. This, however, is a very important term to Luke. It is the way we respond to the gospel so far as he is concerned.[5] John has the idea but he does not use the word. "Believing into the name of Jesus" and "receiving Jesus" are much more his style.[6]

For those of us who are beginners, this is relatively hard work.[7] We should expect that our commentators will help us in these matters. Whatever happens, do not be too proud to use them. This quote is attributed to President Woodrow Wilson: "Use more than the brains you have: use all the brains you can get".[8]

---

5.   Lk 24:47
6.   Jn 1:12
7.   It is for those who are old hands, too!
8.   C. Warne and P. White, *How to Hold an Audience—Without a Rope* (Anzea, 1992) p 10.

The part in the whole revelation

As well as setting the Bible passage into its immediate context and the context of the particular book, we need to be able to set it into the wider context of the Bible itself. We need to ask the question, "How does this fit into the overall message of the Bible?". We do not want it to appear to be different from the overall message that God has revealed to us. This is called 'biblical theology', but don't let the name frighten you! This is what I have described in Chapter 2.[9]

When we do this, the talk should be evangelistic because it will show how the particular part relates to Jesus Christ as Lord and to salvation. However, I have heard sermons on Christian behaviour which seem to be separated from the gospel. I have heard sermons on Ephesians 3-6 as if Chapters 1 and 2 had never been written. Sermons like that will always result in a form of Christian legalism. However, and what is worse, if unbelievers are listening, it will confirm them in their error that getting right with God is a matter of living the good life.

Most people cannot choose the day their friends who do not know Christ will come with them to church. I certainly can't. Their friends generally say which day they will come. I want to be sure that when my friends do come, they will hear the gospel, even if the main thrust of the talk is on Christian behaviour.

---

9.   If you are not familiar with this, may I suggest you read G. Goldsworthy, *Gospel and Kingdom* (Paternoster, 1981) and *According to Plan* (IVP, 1991).

What does the evangelist do?

If what I have said above is correct, then what I do when I am called on specifically to give an evangelistic talk is to look for parts of the Bible that seem to me to be good and simple summaries of the whole. These allow me to speak directly and specifically about the saving Lordship of Jesus. Some examples of these are:

> For God so loved the world that he gave his one and only Son, that whoever believes in him shall not perish but have eternal life.
>
> *(John 3:16)*

> "I am the way and the truth and the life. No one comes to the Father except through me."
>
> *(John 14:6)*

> You see, at just the right time, when we were still powerless, Christ died for the ungodly. Very rarely will anyone die for a righteous man, though for a good man someone might possibly dare to die. But God demonstrates his own love for us in this: While we were still sinners, Christ died for us.
>
> *(Romans 5:6-8)*

> ...I want to remind you of the gospel I preached to you... that Christ died for our sins according to the Scriptures, that he was buried, that he was raised on the third day according to the Scriptures.
>
> *(1 Corinthians 15:1–4)*

> ...God was reconciling the world to himself in Christ, not counting men's sins against them.
>
> *(2 Corinthians 5:19)*

All of the above, in one way or another, take us to the heart of the Bible message.

In addition to the content of the evangelistic talk, there are three other areas that identify it.

1) *Audience*. Although there may be unbelievers and believers present, the evangelistic talk is primarily designed for unbelievers, that they will come to faith in Christ. Others of us will enjoy and be helped by listening, but it is, in the first instance, for them.

2) *Aim*. The aim of the evangelistic talk is to bring the listener to repentance and faith. Material that is extraneous to this must be omitted. The next chapter deals with this.

3) *Style*. Since the talk is for unbelievers, its style should be user-friendly. Jargon and technical terms should be avoided wherever possible and the illustrations should be appropriate for the group to whom you are speaking.

The experience through the Scriptures

Have you ever wondered why Jesus prevented the two walking to Emmaus from recognising him? The Bible says:

> As they talked and discussed these things with each other, Jesus himself came up and walked along with them; but they were kept from recognising him.[10]

Instead, the Lord Jesus teaches them the Bible. You have the strange phenomenon of the author teaching his disciples from his 'autobiography'. When Jesus finally showed them that it was, in fact, he himself and then disappeared, they were not disappointed:

---

10. Lk 24:15–16

> Were not our hearts burning within us, while he talked with us on the road and opened the Scriptures to us?[11]

He had placed into their hands a way of experiencing him whenever they wished it to be so. All they had to do was to return to those Scriptures and their hearts would burn afresh. Had he simply appeared to them, they would probably have hankered for that experience again and again. But he did for them something even better. They could relive it whenever they liked.

I want our preaching in the contemporary setting to be like this. I want us to introduce both adults and children to Jesus by teaching them the Bible. My aim is for people to echo those words: "Were not our hearts burning within us... while he opened the Scriptures to us".

Summary

1. All preaching will be evangelistic to some extent when it is set in its biblical theology, because it will point to Jesus.
2. Specific evangelistic talks have in mind:
    (a) the message of the Bible in a 'nutshell' concerning Jesus;
    (b) the aim that unbelievers will come to repentance and faith;
    (c) that the unbelievers in the audience are our main concern on these occasions; and
    (d) that the style of the talk should be suitable for unbelievers.

---

11. Lk 24:32

CHAPTER FOUR

What is the aim of evangelistic preaching?

What is this chapter about?

1. Our aim in giving evangelistic talks is to present Jesus Christ so that people will respond in repentance and faith.
2. If people respond positively to Jesus as Saviour and Lord, then repentance and faith will follow.

There is an old proverb that says, "He who aims at nothing always hits the target". Never is this more so than in the evangelistic talk. We need to be clear in our mind about the nature of the gospel and what we hope it will do as we preach it.

The gospel we preach

Mark describes the beginning of the Lord Jesus' ministry in these words:

> After John was put in prison, Jesus went into Galilee, proclaiming the good news of God. "The time has come", he said. "The kingdom of God is

near. Repent and believe the good news."[1]

The Lord Jesus was preaching the gospel of God. It is exactly what the apostle Paul believed he was doing. Paul says that he was 'set apart for the gospel of God'.[2] These men did not have a gospel that was peculiar to them. They had not made it up. They had received it.

This gospel, which is the powerful way God saves people,[3] gets its power because it comes from God. He has spoken it.

This may seem an obvious thing to say but, if we take the Bible seriously, we will know that it is possible to have 'another gospel' which is not God's but has its origin with us. That is what the apostle Paul says the Galatians had done.

> I am astonished that you are so quickly deserting
> the one who called you by the grace of Christ and
> are turning to a different gospel—which is really
> no gospel at all.[4]

He also accuses the Corinthians of deserting Jesus, whom he had preached to them, for 'another' Jesus and 'another' gospel which others had told them of.[5] He is very severe in his judgement on other such speakers.[6]

If we are not preaching God's gospel then what we are preaching will be ours or someone else's. We are all tempted to tell people what they want to hear. If we do this, we will never tell them that they are sinners and that

---

1. Mk 1:14
2. Rom 1:1
3. Rom 1:16
4. Gal 1:6–7
5. 2 Cor 11:4
6. Gal 1:9

they are facing the wrath of God in judgement. If we decide that we will always be positive and never negative, we will not face people with the possibility of death and worse. If we make assumptions about what people will and will not listen to instead of being governed by what the word of God says, we will undoubtedly end up with 'another gospel'.

As has been pointed out already, if we use the opportunity that preaching allows to show off and to make a name for ourselves, we will probably 'empty the cross of Christ of its power' and come under the judgement of 1 Corinthians 1:17. It may have been God's gospel but the speaker's self-interest will have nullified it.

If we are people who cannot live without the constant affirmation and adulation of others, we will be tempted to preach another gospel. The early signs of this are that we wait around after the talk to be told how good it was. And we are slightly (or otherwise) hurt if nothing happens. This needs to be recognised and repented of.

The only remedy is to be constantly at prayer that God will give us good understanding of his word and to carefully study that word to see that what we are saying is, in fact, what God is saying in his word, the Bible. It is a serious matter. As well, we should be enlisting our friends to pray for us.

Preaching for response

As we have seen in Chapter 2, Jesus is now both the King and Saviour of God's people. So, the response we are looking for when we preach is that people will come to terms with this reality and act appropriately.

When the apostle Paul writes to the Thessalonians, he tells them that their response to the gospel, which he had preached to them while he was with them, was a model response to others. This is how he described it:

> ...you turned to God from idols to serve the living and true God, and to wait for his Son from heaven, whom he raised from the dead—Jesus who rescues us from the coming wrath.[7]

When Paul addresses the elders from the church at Ephesus, he tells them his aim in preaching. He summed it up in these words:

> I have declared to both Jews and Greeks that they must turn to God in repentance and have faith in our Lord Jesus.[8]

Repentance towards God

God is to be respected and responded to in an appropriate manner. He is to be honoured as King. His appointed King, Jesus, is to be honoured and served. There is no place for idolatry of any form. Equally, self-rule is inappropriate whether it is expressed with passive indifference or active opposition.

I should hasten to say that the rule of God and the Lordship of Jesus are not burdensome. God is a generous ruler. When Jesus calls us to take his yoke upon us, he assures us that his "yoke is easy and his burden is light".[9] Unlike our former ruler, Satan, whose only aim was to destroy us, the true and living God gives us all things for our enjoyment.[10]

---

7.   1 Thess 1:9–10
8.   Acts 20:21
9.   Matt 11:28–29
10. 1 Tim 6:17

This is why his service is perfect freedom. At last we can start to live as God meant us to live.

Such repentance is a way of life where we recognise Jesus as our King and we set out to please him in every area of our life. As we discover more about his character this will bring us to new areas of repentance. This is a lifetime's work. It is part of the dynamic of Christian living.

Some people, at the point of initial repentance, are affected emotionally as they realise the damage they have done to themselves and others in their rebellion against God. For others this is expressed in regret that they had not repented sooner. However it is not how we feel that makes us repentant, but how we intend to live in God's world. It is not a matter of *how I feel* but of *who is in charge*. It is possible to feel sorrow and remorse and never repent. It is possible to repent and not have any strong feeling at all. The story which Jesus told of the two sons who were asked to work in their Father's vineyard, makes this clear.[11] The son who said he would not go, repented and went. It was his going which showed his repentance. We are not told how he felt about the whole deal. He repented. He went. He changed his mind.

Repentance is changing our minds about who is in charge of the world and of our lives, and resolving to live under the rule of Jesus. It is turning to God from idols to serve the true and living God.

Faith in the Lord Jesus

It is one thing to decide that, in the past, we have been mistaken about our allegiance and to decide that, from

---

11. Matt 21:28–32

now on, we will serve Jesus as our Lord. What is to happen about our past? It needs to be dealt with. What of the damage we have done in our rebellion towards God. We need forgiveness. God provides this for us in the death of Jesus. What we are to do is to trust God that he will keep his promise and forgive us because of the death of the Lord Jesus.

In doing this we are to abandon any idea that we can make ourselves acceptable to God. We are totally dependent on the work of Jesus for our acceptability.

Faith is not an ill-defined feeling of wellbeing towards God. Faith is not a feeling at all. Faith is belief that God will do what he has promised to do. It may effect our feelings as may repentance, but they are not of the essence of faith. This is how it is described for us. Speaking of Abraham, Paul says:

> Yet he did not waver through unbelief regarding the promise of God, but was strengthened in his faith and gave glory to God, **being fully persuaded that God had power to do what he had promised**. This is why "it was credited to him as righteousness".[12]

The content of Abraham's faith was that God would keep his promise about Abraham fathering a son. For us the content is different, but the God in whom we trust is still as reliable today as he was in the past. What we are called upon to believe is different from that of Abraham. Paul goes on to describe the content like this:

> The words "it was credited to him" were written not for him alone, but also for us, to whom God

---

12. Rom 4:20–21

will credit righteousness—for us who believe in
him who raised Jesus our Lord from the dead. He
was delivered over to death for our sins and raised
to life for our justification.[13]

It is not the activity of our faith that is important, but in
whom we put our faith. In the past, our trust was in
ourselves or our own goodness, but now we have trans-
ferred our trust to the God who saves us because of the
death of the Lord Jesus.

Repentance and faith go hand in glove. We should not
preach in a way that will enable people to believe that
they can do one without the other. To think that I have
repented without placing my trust in God's promise of
forgiveness would be to replace all the other 'good works'
in which I trusted with repentance. It would be to believe
that I am acceptable to God because I had repented. To
try to exercise faith without repentance would be to think
that I could have forgiveness while I was still in a state of
rebellion towards God. It is just not on.

Preaching Jesus as Saviour and Lord

Repentance and faith should be the logical outcome of
preaching Jesus as King and Saviour.

This should happen when we provide people with the
right *information* and then *persuade them* that this information is both true and reliable and that they should
decide to act accordingly. Evangelistic preaching, like all
preaching, is directed at the will. We want people to
decide to follow Jesus and to bring their lives into align-
ment with God's word.

---

13. Rom 4:23–25

Informing the mind does this. It is done to persuade the person, through information and emotions, to make an act of will. It is not directed to the mind alone or to the emotions alone but to the will through the mind and the emotions.

Jesus is king

When we present people with the fact that Jesus is king they have only two options—to believe it or not to believe it. Negatively they can continue to rebel against him and run their own lives their own way. Such a person might be a good, clean-living person, but that is not the issue. They have failed to recognise his rule over their lives. Alternatively they can 'bow the knee of their lives' and serve Jesus as their Lord.

Jesus is Saviour

Faith acts in exactly the same way. We present the facts about Jesus as Saviour and his sin-bearing death and resurrection. If people act negatively to this and reject it, they will seek to win God's favour in some other way, or they will simply ignore it. If, on the other hand, they act positively to the information we present, they will admit their need for forgiveness and put their trust in the promise of God to forgive them.

What can we expect?

When we preach evangelistically, we are expecting that people will hear the voice of God and will respond. Our confidence that this will happen has nothing to do with our skill in giving information and in persuading people that this is a good way of life for them. Our confidence comes from the gospel itself. This is the powerful way that

God uses to save people. By the Holy Spirit, he opens people's minds to receive the word and to take action.[14] Paul describes the gospel as "the power of God for the salvation of everyone who believes".[15] When people are convinced of this, they will take every opportunity to ensure that their friends hear the good news. When speakers are convinced of this, and believe that the Holy Spirit will open people's minds to receive the word, they will exhibit a calm confidence that "faith comes by hearing" the preaching of Christ.[16]

Repentance and faith—a way of life

Repentance and faith are not just the initial responses we make to the gospel. They are a way of life for the believer. The way we come to Christ is the way we continue. The gospel is as good for believers as it is for unbelievers. When the apostle Paul reminded the elders from Ephesus that he called everyone to repentance and faith, it was not primarily because they were unbelievers. This is the way Christians live. That is why the call to repentance and faith will be a component part of all preaching.

If I was preaching on Luke 18:1–8, which is about praying and not giving up, I would, before the talk ended, call on people to repent of 'giving up' on prayer and to start again. I would also call on them to trust God that he would hear and answer their prayers according to his promise. I would certainly point out (for any unbelievers who might be present) the foolishness of repenting in the

14. 2 Cor 4:6
15. Rom 1:16
16. Rom 10:17

area of prayer if the rest of their lives were typified by rebellion towards God. Equally it should be clear that we should not try to trust God in the area of prayer but not with all the other areas of our life.

In the next chapter, we are going to show how to select material so that we will be able to reach this aim of repentance and faith.

Summary
1. Our aim in evangelistic talks is for people to come to repentance and faith.
2. As we present the Lord Jesus Christ as both Saviour and Lord, this response should occur.

CHAPTER FIVE

What is God's part and our part in preaching?

What is in this Chapter?

1. When we give evangelistic talks we are in partnership with God.
2. We have different roles to play in this work.
3. God's work is to convince the hearers of the truth of the gospel, to convince them of sin and to cause them to repent and put their faith in Jesus as Lord and Saviour.
4. Our work is to tell the gospel to the best of our ability and to pray that God will use it for the salvation of people.

The Psalmist begins Psalm 127 with these words:

> Unless the Lord builds the house, its builders labour in vain. Unless the Lord watches over the city, the watchmen stand guard in vain.

He is simply stating that we are totally dependent on God for everything, not just for salvation, but for every aspect in life. This being the case, it is obvious that it will also be true in preaching.

71

In partnership with God

I have already spoken about the fact that in giving talks there is a human element and also a divine one. We are partners with God in this work.[1] We are not equal partners, but the partnership is real.

It is important to be able to understand our respective roles. If we neglect this we will encounter difficulties.

If we try to do God's work, which is too ridiculous for words, then we will not relate to people as fellow humans but will be under pressure to 'get results'. This may easily cause us to manipulate our hearers in an endeavour to induce repentance and faith. It is short-sighted and out of character for the person who is preaching the gospel to treat others in this manner. It is a denial of the partnership. People are manipulated when they make a decision, in the heat of the moment, but on sober reflection reject it. They often describe what happened as: "I felt that I had no option. I just had to do what he wanted me to do." I have spoken to people who responded to 'appeals' with no idea why they had come forward. This is not always the fault of the evangelist, but sometimes it is.

If, on the other hand, I confuse my work with God's and think he will work no matter what I do, then I will neglect to study the Bible and to pray. I will become careless in preparation. I may even persuade myself that I am being godly in simply trusting the Holy Spirit. Such behaviour is so close to blasphemy that it is frightening. Once again, it is a misunderstanding of the nature of the partnership.

---

1. 1 Cor 3:9; 2 Cor 6:1

God is sovereign in all his creation

The Bible is clear that God is sovereign over everything in his world. He is sovereign in creation, in history, in salvation and in evangelism. He is also responsible for the results that flow from evangelistic preaching. He brings conviction of sin. He opens blind eyes so that people recognise Jesus for who he is. He is the One who gives hearers the gift of repentance and faith so that they turn back to him and cry, "The Lord, he is God!".

If God, for some reason unknown to us, chooses not to do this, then the speaker is unable to bring about these results. We cannot do it by clever argument or by force of personality and we should not try. Why is this so?

Human nature

We need to reflect on the different ways the Bible speaks about the human condition. We are *blind* and cannot see spiritual truths.[2] We need to be *born again* by the Spirit of God or we will never see the kingdom of God.[3] The Bible says that we are *dead* in the spiritual world and need to be brought to life.[4] This is not something we can do ourselves. A corpse cannot bring itself back to life. We are described as *powerless* and in need of being saved,[5] as *lost* and not being able to find the way.[6] We are *enemies of God* and need to be changed into friends.[7]

These are pictorial ways of describing our condition.

---

2. 2 Cor 4:4–6
3. Jn 3:3
4. Eph 2:4–5
5. Rom 5:6
6. Lk 19:10
7. 2 Cor 5:20

There are so many of them and they are so varied that they leave us with only one conclusion, namely, that left to our own devices we will always say 'No' to God unless he changes us.

This truth is taught clearly by the Lord Jesus when he said:

> No-one can come to me unless the Father who has sent me draws him, and I will raise him up at the last day.[8]

People who can rightly call themselves the children of God are those who have been born of God and not of human decision.[9] They have been born again by the Spirit of God, who blows where he will and is not subject to our whims.[10]

God's role in evangelistic preaching

God's role is to open the blind eyes of the hearers. He causes them to recognise that Jesus really is Lord. God raises the spiritually dead so that they speak to him and listen to his voice speaking to them. Through the Holy Spirit, God brings about conviction of sin and causes us to want forgiveness.[11] He gives us faith as a gift[12] so we can trust in the death of the Lord Jesus for our forgiveness and acceptance by God. He gives us repentance as a gift[13] so we can turn around and ask for forgiveness. He is the

---

8. Jn 6:44
9. Jn 1:13
10. Jn 3:3–8
11. Jn 16:8–11
12. Acts 14:27; Eph 2:8
13. Acts 5:31; 11:15–18

74

One who is calling out a people who will live for the praise of his glory.[14]

Our role in evangelistic preaching

Having said this, you may think that there isn't all that much left to do. However our partnership is real and important. God does his work as we do ours. God's word tells us that our new birth was brought about by the "living and enduring word of God" that was preached to us.[15]

Our role is two-fold. We are to preach the gospel and pray. These are the God-given ways he uses to bring people back to himself. He generally does not act independently of us, although he is God and can do as he pleases. He created preaching and prayer for this very purpose.

Our work and God's are well described alongside each other in 2 Corinthians 4:4–6:

> The god of this age has blinded the minds of unbelievers, so that they cannot see the light of the gospel of the glory of Christ, who is the image of God. For we do not preach ourselves, but Jesus Christ as Lord, and ourselves as your servants for Jesus' sake. For God, who said, "Let light shine out of darkness", made his light shine in our hearts to give us the light of the knowledge of the glory of God in the face of Christ.

We preach Jesus Christ as Lord. We do it as 'slaves' of those to whom we preach. God shines the light into people's minds. They recognise Jesus as God and respond appropriately. It is because of this that we beg people to

---

14. Rom 8:28; Eph 1:11–12
15. 1 Pet 1:23–25

be reconciled to God.[16] We urge them to take action because God has commanded everyone everywhere to repent as a judgement day is coming.[17]

This partnership is real

Both partners have a part to play. If we fail to recognise this, we are either frustrated by lack of results or we become lazy in preaching and prayer. This should not be the case.

In Matthew 11, we have a good illustration of the total balance the Lord Jesus had when he spoke evangelistically. He had been working in Korazin, Bethsaida and Capernaum. There he had performed many of his mighty works. No-one repented! It is hard to imagine that. Here we have the finest of speakers and the best of miracle workers and no-one repented. Jesus castigates them for this:

> Woe to you Korazin! Woe to you Bethsaida! If the miracles which were performed in you had been performed in Tyre and Sidon, they would have repented long ago in sackcloth and ashes.[18]

There is no doubt that Jesus thinks they are responsible for their actions. They had good opportunities to respond but they refused. Others would have responded but were not in their position

In his subsequent prayer, Jesus shows his total trust in his heavenly Father for results:

> I praise you, Father, Lord of heaven and earth, because you have hidden these things from the wise

---

16. 2 Cor 5:20
17. Acts 17:30
18. Matt 11:21

and learned, and revealed them to little children.
Yes, Father, for this was your good pleasure.[19]

He rests in the fact that God is sovereign. God hides and
God reveals. No doubt Jesus was sad as the stern warning
shows. It was a tragedy. But bringing about repentance
was in the hands of another, not his.

We might be tempted to believe that such trust will
lead to evangelistic complacency. Not a bit of it! Jesus
presses on with the gospel appeal. "Come to me, all you
who are weary and burdened and I will give you rest."[20]

The knowledge that results are in the hands of God is
wonderfully liberating. It frees us from the pressure of
having to get results and it enables us to preach the gospel
in the best and most efficient way possible. This is illustrated in a passage in Acts 13:48. The Jews at Antioch of
Pisidia reject the gospel, so Paul and Barnabas preach it to
the Gentiles. This is how the Gentiles' response is described:

> When the Gentiles heard this they were glad and
> honoured the word of the Lord; and all who were
> appointed for eternal life believed.

Once again, this knowledge that God had appointed some
to eternal life did not stop them or even deter them from
getting on with their gospel preaching. If anything, it
encouraged them. We read:

> At Iconium Paul and Barnabas went as usual into the
> Jewish synagogue. There they spoke so effectively
> that great numbers of Jews and Gentiles believed.[21]

---

19. Matt 11:25–26
20. It is worth reading the whole section in Matt 11:20–30.
21. Acts 14:1

Prayer a powerful agency

As well as the preaching of the gospel, prayer is another powerful agency that God has created so that we can be co-workers with him.

At the Last Supper, Jesus reminds his disciples of the importance of prayer and the spread of the gospel. These are linked with the coming of the Holy Spirit. He assures them that the work he has been doing in revealing the gospel will be their work as well. Indeed, they will do greater work than he did because he is going to the Father. He assures them that through prayer and the coming of the Holy Spirit they will achieve it.[22] He goes on to teach them that, if they abide in him, the true vine, they will be abundant fruitbearers. Speaking evangelistically is part of this. As well as linking this with the coming of the Spirit, Jesus links it with prayer.[23]

It is completely appropriate to pray because of the spiritual nature of our work. We should pray that we will understand the passage on which we are preaching. We want to understand its meaning. We ask God to enlighten our understanding so that its truth will be clear to us and master us before we teach it to others. This should make us study it harder. We should not reach the stage where we believe that we do not need God's help. Nothing enhances the speaker like humility.

We should be at prayer about the people who will listen to our talk—that God will open their minds and shine the gospel truths into them—that he will give them

---

22. Jn 14:12–17
23. Jn 15:1–17, 26–27. And see D. A. Carson, *Jesus and His Friends* (IVP, 1980).

repentance and faith; that he will do for us what he did for the apostle Paul in Thessalonica. There God worked powerfully and convinced the hearers that what they were hearing was more than the words of a man. They were the words of God.[24] We should be encouraging our friends to pray these things for us and the hearers as well.[25]

There is a fine line between trusting God for results and becoming indifferent to the results of our preaching. When people come to Christ we ought to be ecstatic. When God brings people to repentance and faith we should be filled with awe and wonder that God has worked such a miracle in our midst. This seems to be the way God reacts![26] Both pride and complacency are to be repented of and made a matter of prayer by the speaker.

The Holy Spirit and the speaker

There is no doubt that there is a strong correlation between the work of the Holy Spirit and results that flow from evangelistic talks. He regenerates us and makes us Christ-like. During the preparation, he is with us and helps us. We don't know much about the people we will be speaking to, but he does. He guides us according to their needs because he knows exactly what they are like. He also is the one who powerfully takes the word preached and changes people with it. He is at work in the lives of the Christians who will be bringing their friends to hear what we have to say. Remember that he has been helping them to witness by word and deed to these

---

24. 1 Thess 1:5
25. Col 4:3
26. Lk 15:10

friends. He loves them much more than we do. He will continue to do his work in those who have heard the talk after the event is well and truly over, as they think about it and recall it.

It is a great partnership and we are privileged to be allowed to be part of it.

Conclusion

1. The partnership into which God draws us, as preachers of the gospel should fill us with wonder, awe and humility.
2. This partnership should cause us to work hard at our job of preaching well and to be at prayer.
3. We can trust God to call to himself those whom he will save, and we honour him in this trusting.

CHAPTER SIX

How to select material for evangelistic preaching from Old Testament, Gospels and Epistles

What is in this chapter?
This chapter shows how to select material from different parts of the Bible for the preparation of evangelistic talks.

It is one thing to talk about our aim, and what preaching is all about, and whether every talk is evangelistic. But the time comes when you have to sit down and prepare the talk. The question needs to be answered, "What part of the Bible will I expound so that the gospel will be clear and people will be able to respond appropriately?".

I have already shown that, when we give evangelistic talks, we will expound some part of the Bible. The only question is, "Which part?".

Remember that we are looking for parts of the Bible that capture the 'nutshell'—that Jesus is the Saving Lord.

Some parts select themselves

If you are engaging in expository preaching where you are regularly teaching through books of the Bible, you will notice that, from time to time, certain passages will select themselves. These will enable you to preach the gospel clearly as it comes in the normal event of the preaching programme.

If we were giving a series of talks on Ephesians 1, there is no doubt that the section that contains verses 7 and 11 would be an ideal section on which to speak evangelistically.

I was invited to be a guest speaker at a church recently. They were having a series of talks on the Apostles Creed. I was asked to preach one entitled "I believe in the forgiveness of sins". A special effort had been made by the regular members to bring their non-churchgoing friends for this talk. Since the topic does not come directly from the Bible, I needed to select a Bible passage on it. I remembered that the subject was addressed in 1 John, so I preached on the passage from 1 John 1:8–10. If I could not remember such a passage, I would go to a concordance and look up 'forgiveness' and search though those parts under that heading and select one that said what was required.

One-off evangelistic events

Most of the events you will be likely to speak at will be ones where you will be asked to make a selection of the topic and the passage of scripture that you will expound.

In Chapter 4, we looked at the fact that our aim in the evangelistic talk is to so teach that if people respond positively to the talk, they will repent and put their faith in the Lord Jesus.

I have also pointed out that if we teach that Jesus is

Lord and King in God's world, this should bring about awareness of sin and the need for repentance. We will need to tell people that our sin, in essence, is seen in our rebellion to Jesus as our Lord and to call on them to repent. In addition, we will need to show that Jesus is a Saviour who took the punishment that our sins deserved and that, through this, we can be forgiven.

What we are looking for, then, are parts of the Bible that enable us to do this without stretching their meaning or making them say something which is not really there.

Examples of this can be found in all the parts of the Bible, but my advice for beginners is to look in the Gospels where you will find plenty of material. It will be in narrative form. This is easier for the speaker to tell and much easier for the listener to listen to. It is appealing to the post-modern mind. It will be about the Lord Jesus— who he is and what he has done. We know too, that these stories were what the apostles preached when they were gospelling.[1]

Different parts stress different aspects

Different parts of the Bible stress different aspects of the gospel. Generally speaking, the Gospels show the person of the Lord Jesus more than they explain his work. In the Epistles, we generally have the work of the Lord Jesus explained in detail but less about his person.

In the Old Testament, Jesus is in the 'picture' behind all that is happening. We will need to show that the pattern of God's work before Jesus came was to prepare his people to recognise Jesus when he did come. They had 'seen' him

---

1.   Lk 1:2; Jn 20:30–31

in everything God had been doing in their history.

With this in mind, here are some examples taken from different parts of the Bible.

Examples from the Gospels
a) *Matthew 16:13–23*

1. Who is Jesus really? vv 13–20	He is the Christ.
2. What did he come to do? vv 21–23	To die and rise again.

b) *Mark 4:24–41*

1. Who is this man?	The Lord of the creation.
2. What has he done?	Rescued his people.

c) *Luke 2:11*

1. To you is born a saviour.	
2. The Saviour is Christ the Lord.	

d) *John 10:1–11*

1. Christians are friends with God. v 3	Known by name.
2. Christians follow Jesus as their leader. v 4	
3. Christians are forgiven. v 11	He lays down his life for the sheep.

Some examples from the Epistles
a) 1 Thessalonians 1:9–10
1. They turned to God from idols etc.
2. They waited for his Son etc.

b) Colossians 2:13–15
1. Sins nailed to the cross. vv 13–14
2. He became Lord through this. v 15

An example from Old Testament history
1 Samuel 17:58
1. David is God's appointed King. 1 Sam 16:13
2. David rescues God's people from their enemies.
3. He is like the Lord Jesus who is God's perfect king and who is God's rescuer for us.

An example from Old Testament poetry
Psalm 98
1. The God who saves. vv 1–3
2. The God who is King. vv 4–6
3. The God who is Judge. vv 7–9
4. Jesus is God's appointed Saviour, King and Judge.

An example from the Old Testament prophets
Jeremiah 31:31–34
1. New covenant people—which God will do. vv 31–32
2. New covenant people with changed hearts. v 33
3. New covenant people are friends with God. v 34
4. New covenant people are totally forgiven. v 35
5. Jesus achieves all this through his death on the cross (Luke 22:19–20) and is also all this in his life as the new Israel.

Keep a notebook

When you are asked to preach evangelistically it is not always easy to remember a passage that you read some months ago which, at the time, you thought would be good for evangelism.

My normal Bible reading habit is to try to read the Bible each morning. I usually do this with the aid of a Bible Commentary on the book of the Bible I am then reading. Over the years, I have found it helpful to keep a notebook into which I write Bible references suitable for evangelistic talks like the ones above, which I have noticed as I have been doing my daily Bible reading.

When I have read a part of the Scriptures where I can see that I will be able to show that Jesus is Saviour and Lord, I jot down the reference. I might make a few notes like the ones above. When the time comes to prepare, there are several passages waiting to be prepared. Sometimes when I return, I discover that the passage does not really say what I thought it had. So I scrap it and choose another.

Summary

The Bible offers us a wide variety of different passages from which we can give evangelistic talks. This should lead to wide variety in our preaching.

PART TWO

Servants of the People

(2 CORINTHIANS 4:5)

CHAPTER SEVEN

Preparing the talk: the body of the talk

What is in this chapter?
1. A talk consists of:
   a) an introduction;
   b) the body of the talk; and
   c) the conclusions.
2. The Bible passage dictates the general theme and the supporting ideas for the body of the talk.
3. You should start preparing the body of the talk first.
4. Do this by making the supporting points, showing where you found them in the Bible, and explaining, illustrating and applying them.

We can talk forever about what we are doing, but the time has come to sit down and prepare the talk.

Working at the text
The first, and by far the most important, part of preparation is to make sure that we have understood the text we are going to preach on.

1. Read through the passage several times and make sure you can understand the meaning of all the words. Make a note of any you are unsure of and look them up in your commentaries or in a Bible dictionary. Suppose you are preaching on the story in Luke 7:36–50 of the 'sinful' woman who washes Jesus' feet with her tears. You notice that Jesus has been invited to the home of a Pharisee. Do you know who Pharisees are? Where will you get this information? In your Bible Dictionary[1] look up "Pharisee". You will find an extensive article. You may or may not use this material in the talk, but you do need to know it before you proceed.

As you continue to read, you find the woman is described as "having lived a sinful life in that town". Does that strike you as strange? Isn't everyone like that? So what does it mean? You may have an idea but you would be wise to go to your commentaries and check your understanding.

2. Start to ask questions of the passage.
What is the main point of this story?
Who are the important characters?
Why are they important?
Why was the story written in the first place?
Would it matter if it were not there?
What other parts of the Bible are like it?

These questions are designed to help us think carefully about the passage and to be clear about its meaning. As you do this and as you read the commentaries, you will accumulate a considerable amount of material which will

---

1. I recommend *The New Bible Dictionary* (IVP).

reflect the questions that have appealed to you as important and interesting. Many of them, and their answers, will be discarded as the talk takes shape. You will find this hard at the beginning because all the material is so good. You will have had such a good time reading and collecting it that it is nearly impossible to discard any of it.

Working on packaging the talk

When you think you know what the passage means, you now have to organise the talk into some form for its presentation. We want it to be clear, easy to follow, interesting, appealing and challenging.

The talk is made up of three parts:
    The Introduction
    The Body
    The Conclusion

Although the introduction is the first part of the talk to be given, it is the last part to be written down. This gives you the maximum amount of time to think about it.

The 'shape' of the talk

Now that you have studied the passage, ask yourself the question, "What is the big idea in this passage"?[2] This should be able to be written down in one sentence. It will be the aim of the talk. It is what you hope your hearers will have learnt from the passage when the talk is finished.

As I am writing this, I am in the process of preparing a talk for Christmas on Matthew 1:18–23. I have spent a

---

2.   See Haddon Robinson *Biblical Preaching* (Baker, 1988), Chapter 2, and J Stott *I Believe in Preaching* p 224ff.

considerable amount of time studying this passage and I think that the 'big idea' is that:

Jesus forgives the sins of his people by becoming Immanuel, God with us, for them.

The big idea is always arrived at by studying the passage and it should not be imposed on the passage. The Bible should dictate what we will say and not the reverse.

Having arrived at the big idea, I now go back to the passage to provide the evidence that convinced me that this was, in fact, the big idea.

In the talk I am preparing, I go back to the passage and note:

1. From verse 21—that the child will be called Jesus because he will save his people from their sins. .

2. From verse 23—that all this was to fulfil the prophecy that God would be with his people (Immanuel).

These are the reasons why I concluded that the big idea was as I have stated. And thus they are also the reasons that I should point out to my hearers, so that they will be as convinced as I was.

So this talk will have two points:

1. Jesus saves his people from their sin; and
2. Jesus is Immanuel.

It is important to note that it is through the study of the Bible passage that we arrive at both the big idea and the supporting ideas.

The body of the talk

Having arrived at the points we want to make, the next step is to ask what to do with them.

Here is a simple outline that will give you better than average results fairly quickly. It isn't the only way to

organise material, but it is a good one.
1. State the point (what is it that you want to say).
2. Show me where you found it in the Bible.
3. Explain it (tell me what it means).
4. Illustrate it (show me what it is like).
5. Apply it (Tell me what to do with it).

Having done this with main point 1, proceed to the next main point and do the same again. Let me tease out how each of these steps works.

1. State the point

This should be done memorably and briefly. It is not only designed to focus attention, but to provide a 'hook' for people to remember the talk afterwards.

In the example above I have stated the points as:
1. Jesus saves his people from their sins;
2. Jesus is Immanuel, God with us.

While these are accurate, they are not very memorable. So I begin to 'play' with these ideas to see if I can state them in a better way. How about:

"There are two aspects about Christmas worth noting:
1. Jesus is **God For Us**; and
2. Jesus is **God With Us**."

Another could be:
"This part of the Bible draws our attention to two important aspects of Christmas:
1. **Forgiveness from God**; and
2. **Friendship with God**."

Or just:
"1. **Forgiveness**; and
2. **Friendship**."

During the course of the rest of the preparation I will keep thinking about these headings and I will experiment with a variety until I arrive at those that I think will be easily understood and easily remembered. I say them aloud to see how they 'sound'. I put them on tape and listen to them. I see which one has the biggest impact.

As you write out the talk, these headings will be underlined or shown in bold or a different colour.

When you come to speak these headings as you deliver the talk, you will need to orally 'underline' them. This can be done with words such as, "The first thing I want to draw to your attention etc." Or it can be done with your voice, or both. You can state the point by raising the volume of your voice or conversely you can lower it. You can speak slowly and deliberately or you can speed it up. But whatever you do, do not state the point in exactly the way you say every-thing else. Why not try out some variations on a tape and see what they sound like.

The use of the 'pause' can be helpful. For example, "The first thing I want to say is (*pause*) that Christmas is about 'Forgiveness'".

Remember—the point must be:

Easy to grasp.

Easy to understand.

Easy to remember.

2. Show me in the Bible

Having stated the point, you now need to show your listen-ers where you found it in the Bible. I don't think a talk is a sort of meditation where the Bible passage is read at the beginning but never referred to again during the talk. The dynamic of giving talks from the Bible is not so much that I, the speaker, tell you, the listener, what the Bible is saying. It is rather that I, the speaker, invite you, the listener, to look at the Bible with me and together we discover its meaning.

It is highly likely that at most evangelistic gatherings people will not have their Bibles with them. In any case, they may not be able to look up Bible passages with ease. It is a good idea to have the organisers print the Bible passage so that people will be able to read it as it is being read aloud, and refer to it later. The Bible passage could be:

a) printed on a card and distributed just before the talk; or

b) printed on the insides of menus or programmes; or

c) printed on place mats at a dinner.

It is sometimes possible for a copy of a Gospel from which you are preaching to be given out so that everyone has the same version. These are not costly and can be obtained from the Bible societies.

When directing people's attention to the Bible passage, tell them the page number and the paragraph or sentence number rather than by referring to chapters and verses. I would say something like, "This booklet is part of the Bible. Luke wrote it. The part I am going to read is on page 10 at the sentence numbered 32."

OK. Let's return to our talk. It is beginning to look like this:

"The first thing I want to say is that **Christmas is about forgiveness**. Please look at the sentence numbered 21 and you will see what I mean."

You now have two options. You can pause while they read it, or you can read it aloud. It is probably good to do both. You can then be sure that everyone has finished and those who, for one reason or another, have not read it will have heard it.

3. Explain it

The next thing to do is to explain what the point you have made means.

Here you will have the material you have already researched at your fingertips. It is time now to sort out what needs to be said and what can be discarded.

As you are writing out these explanations, it is worth bearing in mind that we speak differently from how we write. Written communication allows us to have the maximum amount of ideas with the minimum amount of words. People can read them at their leisure. They can stop and think. They can re-read them and, if they are eager beavers, they can look up the meaning of words in a dictionary!

This is not the case with the spoken word. Once it is gone, it is gone. There is no time to stop and think about an idea. The speaker needs to leave 'time' for that thinking to be done while speaking. That means the idea will be re-stated. Shorter sentences are more easily grasped than long and complicated ones. As you are writing the manuscript, ask yourself the question, "Is this the way I speak?". Say the sentences to your computer or to the page you are writing on. Listen to how they sound. See if there is an easier way for the listener to grasp it quickly. Every minute you spend doing this is invaluable.

Let's return to the sample talk I have been preparing for Christmas on Matthew 1:18-23. I have made the point—**Christmas is about Forgiveness.** I have read verse 21—"She will give birth to a son and you will give him the name Jesus, because he will save his people from their sins".

I now need to explain the point. So I say:

When I say that Christmas is about forgiveness I

don't mean that I should forgive you, or you me, however important that might be. I am talking about God forgiving you and me. That forgiveness!

There are two accounts of the birth of the Lord Jesus. This one tells us about how Joseph, the 'father' of Jesus, felt when he discovered that his fiancée was pregnant.

Marriage regulations are very different as you move around the world. A friend of mine told me that he was at a wedding in India where the groom made a speech in which he thanked his parents for going to so much trouble in choosing the wife they had for him. And how pleased he was with their choice. It's hard for us in the West to think of someone else choosing a wife or a husband for us.

At the time of Jesus, people entered into formal engagements before they married. It was binding. It could not be dissolved or broken except through legal 'divorce'.

In the part of the Bible we have read, we see that Joseph is in a bind.

He is engaged to Mary.

He loves her.

He is a godly man.

He always tried to do the right thing.

He discovers that she is pregnant. We don't know whether this is because Mary has told him or whether it has now become apparent. He can see for himself.

He knows that he is not the father.

He has only one option open.

He will have to annul the engagement.

While he is thinking about this, an angel appears to him in a dream. The angel is a messenger from God.

God tells him what is going on.

We don't know why Mary had not told him. Perhaps it was because she was too modest. Or it may have been that she just didn't think that Joseph would believe her. I don't blame her. Would you believe it if your fiancée told you that she was pregnant by a supernatural intervention of the Holy Spirit?

Whatever the reason, we know that he had assumed unfaithfulness on her part.

However, Joseph is caught up in something momentous. He is swept up into the plan of God for saving the world. The village carpenter is to become the father of the Son of God.

What a dream that was!!

"You will call his name Jesus because he will save his people from their sins."

The Jews had waited a long time for their saviour to come. Thousands of years before, God had made a promise that he would send them a king. This king would save them from their sins and rule them in such a way that justice and peace would always happen. Joseph discovered that he was caught up in this wonderful process.

I need to interrupt this story with some explanations. If Jesus is to save people from their sins we will need to be clear what we mean by 'sins' and what we mean by 'saving'.

I remember reading about a man who saw a sign on which was written, "Jesus Saves". He said to himself, "What a good idea. I ought to be thrifty too."

When I taught kindergarten children, they often told me that Jesus saved their sins. I had a feeling that it was like a hobby. Some people saved stamps but he saved sins.

Sins are as misunderstood as anything I know. When I say that you are a sinful person, I am not making a character statement about you. I am not saying that you are a bad person.

What I am saying is that the Bible says that we have all said 'No' to God as God. We don't want him to be in charge of our lives. We might believe in God and even say our prayers. But we just want God to let us 'run free'. We don't want God to be God, at least over us.

I might be a really nice person and act like this or I could be a complete rat-bag and still not have God as *my* God. I might be a regular church-goer or I might be a self-confessed atheist.

Whatever. We have all said "No" to God as *our* God. This is what the Bible calls 'sin'. And all of us are the same in this regard.

Notice that at this point, although I am talking about sin and forgiveness, I am also really talking about the Lord-ship of Christ. Sin is rebellion against his kingly rule, and repentance is turning back to submit to his kingly rule. Repentance and forgiveness are closely tied together. But to continue...

This attitude of life is very damaging. When we reject God as God, we, ourselves, take over the role. We set ourselves up as God.

This is very destructive behaviour. You see, if I am pretending to be God and you are pretending to be God, when we meet together which one of us will be God? This puts us on a collision course with each other. We can't live with each other properly. The Bible says that this behaviour is the cause of all our problems. We don't relate to God properly. We don't relate to one another properly and we don't relate to the environment properly.

I guess it may not matter all that much if it wasn't for the fact that God has not lost interest in his world. In fact the very opposite. He is passionately concerned about it.

How I treat you matters to God. How I treat God matters to God, and how I treat the world around me matters to God. He says we will be held accountable for this behaviour.

Since we are all sinners, in the way I have explained, we all need forgiveness.

That is what Christmas is all about. **Christmas is about forgiveness.**

And Jesus is the one who brings that forgiveness.

All of us love the baby in the manger, although I suspect we may not have loved the setting all that much if we had been there. However, the baby grew up to manhood. He demonstrated that he was indeed God's King and he climaxed that by dying on the cross. He did that to take the punishment that our sins deserved. He said that his death was for the forgiveness of our sins. On one occasion he said, "I have come...to give my life as a ransom for many".

In your mind please picture Jesus on the cross. You will have seen paintings of this. There is Jesus in the middle, a thief on either side, soldiers and women around the foot of the cross. Listen! Jesus is speaking, "My God! My God! Why have you forsaken me?".

What's going on? Isn't he the Son of God? How can he be God-forsaken?

The Bible says that "he who was without sin was made sin for us so that we might be made righteous". Jesus took the punishment that our sins deserved so that we could be right-with-God.

That is why his name was to be Jesus. It means a Saviour. Because he saves his people from their sins.

No wonder the angel described his message as good news of great joy for all people.

It **is** good news. **Christmas is about forgiveness.**

Did you note that:

1. Although there is structure in the talk, and I will be making two points, the narrative needs to be told again. I assume that the Bible reading would have been done just prior to the talk or after the introduction (more on this in Chapter 9 on 'Introductions'). However I do not want to destroy the story line of the narrative by the structure. I want the structure to serve the narrative.

2. I do not want to give the impression that the talk I have written above would have come out like that the first time I wrote it. I would do it and then re-read it and revise it. This process may happen many times. As I do so, I'm asking questions like: "How can I explain this better?" and "Can I explain this in an easier way?" and "What will bring this to life?".

3. When giving the background material, I tried not to say any more than was necessary so that the rest of the talk could be understood.

4. A great deal of material that I gathered up during my study of the Bible, such as the marriage regulations in Numbers 5:11-13, or that unfaithfulness could well have resulted in stoning from Deuteronomy 22:13–21, and much more, ended up not being used. I don't fret over this. It wasn't a waste of time. It not

only helped me to understand the passage and to clarify what I wanted to say but it also gave me a 'feel' for the situation as I was telling the story.

So far so good. We have:

Stated the point.

Shown where to find it in the Bible.

Explained it.

Now we need to...

4. Illustrate the point

In the following chapter, I will say why I think illustrations matter and how to choose them. All I intend to do here is to show a sample one for the talk I have been preparing for Christmas.

You will remember that the last line of the explanation was:

It is good news. **Christmas is about forgiveness.**

So then I say:

Several years ago I was surfing at Avoca on the central coast of NSW. It was a beautiful day. However the waves were breaking out further than I normally swim. I am talking about body surfing. I had been treading water for several minutes when a wonderful wave came along. It was one of those ones you dream about. The wave was curling around my cheeks and I was rocketing towards the beach. When I had finished—it was so good I decided to go out again for just one more.

I had been treading water for about five minutes when I glanced over my shoulder and noticed that the beach had drifted quite a long way. "Old man", I said, "you had better swim back to shore". I did what it says in the textbook. I didn't panic. I swam steadily to the beach. After what seemed like forever, I flipped onto my back to rest and noticed that I was slightly further out than when I had started to swim back. I tried not to panic! Just then a head bobbed up in front of me in the surf.

"Are you all right, sport?" it said.

"No", was the reply.

"Do you need a hand?"

"Yes please."

"Give me your hand and we'll work together."

I did. He did the man-sized part of the work.

After forever, my feet hit the sand at the bottom. What a great feeling that was! I had been rescued. I had been saved.

The rescue that Jesus brings is a far more important one than this. He brings a permanent rescue from the consequences of my sin.

Finally, we need to...

5. Apply it

So I say:

Do you know what it is to be forgiven? By God, I mean.

Do you know what it feels like? To feel clean inside and wanted by God?

That is what Christmas is about.

You may have missed out in the past. If that is so, please don't let this Christmas slip past without getting this matter settled.

Have a real Christmas and not just a pretend one.

Christmas is about forgiveness.

This brings us to the end of the first point. I would do the same with the second point and any subsequent points.

Although I have two points in the talk I have been using as a demonstration, it doesn't mean that they will both get the same length of time. If one is more important than the other, then it will get the greater attention.

Summary
1. The body of the talk is prepared first.
2. Its main theme and its supporting ideas are found by studying the Bible passage selected for the talk.
3. Each supporting idea is:
   a) stated;
   b) identified in the Bible passage;
   c) explained;
   d) illustrated; and
   e) applied.

CHAPTER EIGHT

Preparing the talk: the use of illustrations

What is in this chapter?

1. The purpose of using illustrations.
2. When it is appropriate and inappropriate to use illustrations.
3. Different types of illustrations.
4. Where illustrations can be found.
5. Variety in illustrations.
6. How to store illustrations for further use.

Up to this point in the preparation of the talk, much of what I have been saying about explaining a passage from the Bible will be appropriate irrespective of the kind of audience. However, when we come to the introduction and the illustrations, it is important that we should be particularly aware of the culture of our audience. We should be asking questions like: "How do they think?", "What are their interests?", "What are their values, hopes and fears?". The cultural background will change with differences in age, place and socio-economic background. An illustration that is completely appropriate for one group may well be inappropriate for another.

The purpose of the illustration

When illustrations are used well they can perform many functions in the talk.

1. *They help to clarify an explanation.* After a well-chosen illustration the hearer may well say, "Thank you. I wasn't sure what you meant, but now I can see clearly what you are on about."

2. *They reinforce an explanation.* On such an occasion a person will say, "I thought that I had understood what you were saying, but now I am sure about it."

3. *They arouse interest and recall attention.* Often a person's interest, which may have been wandering, can be called back by the giving of an illustration.

4. *They allow the listener time to relax and have a rest.* The level of concentration needed to listen to an illustration seems less than when the explanation of the meaning of the text is being done.

5. *They show something of the speaker.* The choice and use of illustrations often gives the hearer some insights into the character of the speaker. This is specially so if, in the use of humour, the speaker tells an illustration against himself or herself.

6. *They allow an appeal to the emotions as well as to the mind.* While factual information and abstract ideas are generally addressed to the mind, an illustration can involve our emotions and so increase the overall effect of the talk, which is always aimed at the will.

7. *They recognise the various learning styles in the members of the audience.* One person will learn better from an illustration, while another learns from a set of propositions.

Illustrations fail when...

If I am correct in what I have said above, it stands to reason that illustrations fail when:

1. *They do not illustrate the point that is being made.* Nothing could be worse than for the people listening to be saying, inside their heads, "I thought that I had understood what he meant, but now I'm not sure if I have understood it at all". It would be better never to use illustrations than for this to happen.

2. *They are inaccurate and distract.* Have you ever had the frustration of not being sure that what has been said is accurate and you spend time trying to work it out? The talk then moves on and you are left high and dry. I remember hearing someone say in a talk, "The Second World War finished in the August of 1944".

I thought, "That can't be right. I remember that I was in the third year at High School. We were allowed home from school early. Church bells were ringing. Someone had fixed a rope to the bell at St Paul's church at Oatley so that anyone who walked by could give it a ring. I was fifteen so it must have been 1945." Meanwhile the talk had advanced quite a pace and left me well behind.

3. *They are so vivid that they overshadow the point being made.* The last thing we want is for the illustration to be remembered and the point it illustrates to be forgotten. This can happen if the illustration is too vivid or if it opens up complex issues that are incidental to the point being illustrated.

For some time I used an illustration about a car accident I was involved in. It went as follows.

> One day a young man ran up the back of my car.
> When I made inquiries I discovered that he didn't

have a license because he was only 15 years old. He told me that the man next door to him had lent him the car to drive down to the corner and come back again so he could 'show-off' to the girl with him. He asked me not to get the police. He assured me that he had not stolen the car and that it wouldn't happen again.

What was I to do? The boot of my car was crumpled up like tissue paper. The 'beaten up' Holden he was driving hardly had a scratch on the bull-bar.

I could let him off and pay for the damage myself.

I could take him back home and see if his father would make good the damage.

I could get the police—have him charged—and make an insurance claim.

However one thing is crystal clear. If my car was to be made good, someone had to pay.

Now it is exactly the same with the damage I have done when I sin. Who will make good the damage I have done there? Damage to myself, damage to other people, damage to the environment and damage to the person of God himself?

The wonderful truth is that the Lord Jesus has paid the full penalty that we deserve for our sins. We can be forgiven totally and start again.

When I used this illustration I was regularly asked the question, "What did you do with the boy?". The story was too vivid and opened up other complex issues such that the death of Jesus was forgotten in this real life drama of the teenager and the car. It was fun while it lasted but useless as an illustration.

It is worth saying that illustrating a minor point in the

talk with a vivid illustration can cause such a distraction that it overshadows the major points you are making. Use the biggest and best illustration for the most important point.

4. *They are used as substitutes for careful explanations of the Bible.* Story telling should not be used as a substitute for carefully explaining the Bible. I have heard talks where the illustration immediately follows the Bible passage quoted without explanation. They make me feel that the speaker lacks confidence in the Bible to be effective and the subsequent explanation seems less important than the story.

5. *There are just too many!* Too many illustrations will highjack the talk. It will become a series of stories loosely strung together around a passage of the Bible. As with too vivid illustrations that people remember rather than the point illustrated, too many illustrations can obscure the message of the Bible passage.

Variety in illustration

There is a wide variety of illustrative material. The most obvious is the story and the most neglected is the vivid use of language. Warne and White have an excellent section dealing with how choosing the right word can make all the difference:

> Precise words give your listener a clear picture; vague words produce hazy pictures. Take the sentence, 'The dwelling was beside the water'. **Dwelling** is a vague word. Precise words are **hut, hovel, mansion,** or **thatched cottage.**
>
> **Water** is a vague word. Precise words are **sea, creek, lake, river,** or **rapids.** Choose precise words so that people will see what you have in mind. Don't

say **animal** if you mean **dog**. And why say **dog** if you mean **bloodhound, poodle,** or **fox terrier?**

Use pictorial nouns. Nouns name things, places, and peoples: pictorial nouns are specific. **Lollies** is a noun. **Toffees, peppermints**, and **jelly-beans** are pictorial nouns.

Use descriptive verbs. Verbs tell what happens; they tell us what the nouns do. Descriptive verbs are specific; they picture vivid action. **Walk** is a verb. **March, stagger, saunter, shuffle**, and **limp**, are descriptive verbs.[1]

One–liners

A single illustrative sentence can re-enforce an idea as easily as a story. I remember reading in Spurgeon[2] a lecture he gave to students training for the ministry. The lecture was on the qualifications needed for a good speaker. He had made the point that the first qualification needed was that the speaker should be converted. He memorably pointed out that to have an unconverted speaker was like having a blind professor of optics or a deaf professor of music.

The story

By far the most common illustration is the story. Stories are good because when they are told well they serve the dual functions of illustrating and attention grabbing. Everyone loves hearing stories, especially when they are told well.

Stories can be fictional or from real life. They may have happened to you or you may have read them or heard

---

1. Warne and White, *How to hold an audience without a rope* pp 33–34.
2. Charles H. Spurgeon, *Lectures to My Students* (Ministry Resources, 1954)

others relate them. Make it clear whether the stories are true or not. Whatever happens, don't make them sound as if you were there when you weren't and don't tell the stories where you are the hero. Nothing irritates Australians more than this. On the other hand, you may tell stories against yourself—they love that!

Sources of illustrations

The Bible is full of stories that serve as excellent illustrations. For the most part, unbelievers are fairly ignorant of the content of the Bible so it is not good merely to make a biblical allusion or reference. You will have to tell the whole story.

Evangelistic books are often made up of collections of talks and are a good source of illustrations.[3]

In *No Wonder They Call Him Savior,* for example, Max Lucado tells a very moving story about a village girl from Brazil who travels to the big city and falls into prostitution.[4] Her distraught mother follows her and begins a search, leaving small photos of herself taped to mirrors and attached to notice-boards throughout the red-light district.

In time, the hurt and disillusioned daughter sees one of the photos and reads the message on the back. It says, "Whatever you've done, whatever you have become, it doesn't matter. Please come home." And she does.

I have heard this story told at length on several occasions in sermons—told rather than read. On every occasion I have been very moved. I have never heard it read

3. J. Chapman, *A Fresh Start* (Matthias Media 1998)
4. Max Lucado, *No Wonder They Call Him Savior* (Multnomah Press, 1986)

aloud (for example, out of Max Lucado's book), and I fancy that it would not be as powerful that way. Perhaps that is because most stories I hear read in talks are read so badly. If you do read stories while speaking, they need to be prepared carefully and well practised. My advice on this one would be to tell it. Its length is an added difficulty, but it is so powerful that I would use it. It would be wonderful to use for Luke 15!

However, if I was quoting some factual event from a newspaper story, I would make a point of reading it out. Reading it highlights the factual nature of the illustration.

In 1998, the Australian Broadcasting Corporation showed a program called *The Invincibles*. It was a documentary about the Australian Cricket Team that visited England in 1948. They were undefeated in the entire tour. This was a record at the time and is still unbroken. Many of the players are still alive and they were interviewed. Clips of the matches played were also shown. At 19, Neil Harvey was the youngest member of that team. Commenting on his first test century, Sam Loxton, who was batting with him, had this to say:

> It was probably the proudest moment on that tour,
> so far as I was concerned, to be batting with him
> (Neil Harvey) when he achieved such success.

I have made a note of this and will use it when I next preach on Philippians 2:3. It illustrates so well the idea of being mindful of others and counting them better than myself.

The use of humour

If you are a person whose sense of humour is well developed it will be unlikely that you will give a talk without some humour. Telling funny stories can be learned, but it has nothing to do with effective speaking. A student, who said to me that he thought that he would not be an effective evangelist because he couldn't tell funny stories, really worried me. Telling jokes has nothing to do with the gospel. People can speak well, be persuasive, and winsome without ever telling a joke.

However, if you are a funny person, you need to take care that you do not do this for its sake or yours. You need to be disciplined in its use.

Whatever we do, we do not want to give the impression that we are flippant about God, the seriousness of the gospel, sin or judgement. Humour, like every other part of the talk, must serve the aim of the talk.

I have seen humour at its best when it has been used to get the audience to laugh at the speaker and themselves.

Like most things, it is a good servant and a pain in the neck when it is the master!

Preparing illustrations for your manuscript

Whether you speak from a full manuscript or from notes, illustrations will need to be written out in the first instance. Try not to tell 'off the cuff' stories. They generally take longer than if you had written them out and practised them. When you come to make your notes, you do not need to write out the whole illustration. You could find it helpful to highlight them in your notes for quick identification.

Collecting and making up illustrations

As you can see from what I have written, I collect illustrations from anywhere. Newspapers, TV, books and real life situations provide a great store for illustrations. I remember hearing Dick Lucas, from Bishopsgate in London, speak at a Church Missionary Society Summer School. He had arrived from London the day before and had had a stopover at Singapore while the plane was refuelling. He spoke on John 2 about the miracle of the water turned into wine. The exposition lasted for 45 minutes during which time he used 15 illustrations. Each one was appropriate and they were well spaced throughout the talk. What was of interest to me was that three of them had been gleaned while he was walking through the airport at Singapore. I realised that for this great speaker, all of life's experience could be the source of illustrations.

Some people store illustrations on card systems or in their database, cataloguing them under subject headings and verses from the Bible.

There is great value in preparing well in advance of the time the talk is to be delivered. This is specially so when it comes to choosing illustrations. If you start early, the talk will be 'on your mind' and it is likely you will see something on TV or in the paper or in your experience that will illustrate something in the talk.

Remember your audience when you choose illustrations

When you are speaking to a mixed audience with men and women of varying ages, background and interests, try to vary the type of illustration. Don't have all the illustrations about sport, the movies or music. Try to appeal to the different interest groups that are present. You would be wise not to quote an article from *Time Magazine* or *The Guardian* when the hearers never read anything except the tabloids.

Books of illustrations and quotes

I have often been asked about the use of these. There are a variety of them available. For my part I have found that there is a lot of material that needs to be read in order to find an appropriate one. I prefer the 'real life' ones which you have directly experienced. They are generally told in a much more vivid way.

Summary
1. Illustrations are very good servants but bad masters.
2. When used well, illustrations bring variety and colour to a talk so that the message of the Bible passage that is being taught is clear and compelling.

CHAPTER NINE

Preparing the talk: the conclusion and the introduction

What is in this chapter?
1. The content of the conclusion.
2. A sample conclusion.
3. The importance of the introduction.
4. Some suggestions for introductions.

We now have the body of the talk written out and all that remains to be done is to write the conclusion and the introduction. The introduction is left until last. This gives us the maximum time to think about it. If the talk is prepared over a period of several days (you may spend a couple of hours a day over the week), you will have the opportunity to think about the introduction at other times, such as driving in the car, when you are washing up, or under the shower. I try them out aloud to see what they 'sound' like.

Arriving at the content of the conclusion
For evangelistic talks, the conclusion is nearly always the same. We have already seen in Chapter 4 that the aim of the evangelistic talk is to bring people to repentance and

faith. The conclusion should do this.

If you have followed the suggested way of constructing the body of the talk, you will already have applied the material you have been teaching in the two or three points that you have made.

In the sample talk I have been using on Matthew 1:18–23, you will remember that there were two points in it:

1. Christmas is about Forgiveness – v21
2. Christmas is about Friendship – v23

You will recall that I applied them in the following way:

Application 1
The reason why Christ died is so that our sins can be forgiven. Christmas is about forgiveness. Do you know this experience? Do you know what it is to be forgiven by God? To be accepted? To be made clean inside? To be wanted? Maybe Christmas has passed you by in the past and its true meaning has never become real in your life. Today is a good day for you to say "Yes" to forgiveness from God and to put your trust in the fact that God will forgive you because of Jesus.

Application 2
It is because Jesus is a Saviour that we can know in reality the presence of God with us all the time; that he is our God here and now. Not just at a special time of religious ecstasy but all the time. We can know his friendship in everyday life: in good times and in bad, in sorrow and in joy, when things are going well, and when 'the wheel is properly off the bike'. For me this is one of the best parts of being a Christian. To know the presence of Immanuel—God with us—and to love and serve him each day. Whatever happens this Christmas, see that you don't miss out on this.

When the applications have been made like this, all that needs to be done is to 'gather up' the applications and re-state them and urge people to take action. This is how I would do that with the sample talk:

Conclusion

To conclude: Christmas is about forgiveness and friendship. Forgiveness from God because Jesus has died for us, and friendship with God because forgiveness now makes this possible. No wonder Christmas is such a good time! A time to say "thank you" to God for such a great gift. It is possible, as you have been listening to me, that you have said to yourself, "I don't really know God as a friend and I certainly don't know what it is to be forgiven". Tonight would be a good night for you to turn back to God and rectify this situation. I will pray a prayer that would be appropriate for you. You might like to echo it to God, in your head, after me. Let me tell you what I will say in the prayer and it will give you time to think. I will say:

> "Dear Heavenly Father, I haven't been serving you as my God and I am sorry about that. From tonight onwards I want to serve you. Please help me. Lord Jesus thank you for dying for me. Please forgive me. Please come and take over the running of my life."

It is important to resist the temptation to re-preach the talk. The conclusion is designed to gather up the main ideas and to call for action. The value of having made the applications through the talk alleviates having to do it at the end. When the body of the talk has ended and you have reached the climax of what you want to say, draw the talk to its end thoughtfully and as quickly as possible

Do not introduce new ideas in the conclusion and do not introduce an illustration here. What information has not been dealt with already cannot be included in this talk.

In the conclusion to the evangelistic talk, the prayer will always have a repentance and faith component. You will see this illustrated in the prayer above:

> *Repentance:*
> Dear Heavenly Father, I haven't been serving you as my God. I am sorry about that. From tonight onwards I want to serve you. Please help me.
>
> *Faith:*
> Lord Jesus, thank you for dying for me. Please forgive me. Please take over the running of my life.

Just as I have advised you to have the Bible passage printed so that people can follow along, so the prayer could be printed on the handout.

Keep the prayer brief and to the point. Don't start another talk in the prayer.

If you pray the prayer and you ask people to pray it after you, make sure you leave enough time for them to do this. I was greeting people at the door after having preached one morning. A man in his early twenties told me that he had enjoyed the talk and that it had greatly helped him. I asked him if he had prayed to receive Christ that morning. His reply startled me.

"Sort of", he said.

"What do you mean, sort of?" was my reply.

"Well I began to pray each sentence but before I had finished you started the next one and I didn't complete any sentence except the last", he said.

"You need an evangelist like me like a hole in the

head", was all I could think to say.

"Why don't we find a quiet corner and do it properly", he requested.

So we did.

Painful isn't it? To overcome this I have adopted the following method. Say the first sentence quickly so that people can 'get it all'. Then say it again slowly inside your head so you know that people have had enough time to repeat it for themselves. Then proceed to the next sentence until you have finished. It is important that the sentences are short and easily remembered.

The introduction

I have already explained that, although this is the first part of the talk to be spoken, it is the last part to be written down. This gives us the maximum time to think about it so that it will achieve its purpose.

The purpose of the introduction is:

1. *To arouse interest and motivate.* Do not take for granted that people will want to listen to what you have to say. They may be distracted by activities that took place before they came to the meeting. They may be apprehensive about what is to take place. Are they going to be asked to stand up? Will they be embarrassed? Will they be bored out of their brains?

The task of the speaker is to overcome these concerns (and even more) in the first few sentences.

2. *To set people at ease.* The first few sentences should give the audience the impression that the speaker knows what he or she is on about, that this will be interesting and that they can relax and know that it will be a helpful time.

3. *To get to know the speaker.* If you are a stranger to the people, they will make some assessment of you from

your first few sentences. Tell them, briefly, why you are glad you are there and that you are glad they are there. If you can get the organisers of the event to have a slot where you can be interviewed before the talk, it saves a great deal of time in the introduction and gives you a running start.

4. *To introduce the subject of the talk.* The introduction sets the scene for the beginning of the 'big idea'. When I have finished introducing the talk, my hope is that people are saying to themselves, "I'm really glad I didn't sleep in. That is exactly what I want to know. Please tell me how this talk will do me good and why I should listen to it for the next 20 minutes."

The talk has begun with the first words that the speaker speaks. It stands to reason that introductions like —"Luke 7:31. Please open your Bible at page 734. You will find an outline of the talk on the notice sheet."—are not good enough. As I listen to them, I am trying to work out if it will be worth the effort.

Leave these practicalities until you have motivated your hearers. They will then want to do what you are asking them to do. Speakers do this to clear the decks so *they* can get started. It has very little to do with the hearers and what they want. Need I say that this is a totally inappropriate time to give out notices that have been forgotten or overlooked elsewhere?

How to do it [1]
There are several ways in which the introduction may be commenced:

---

1. Much of the material in this section is indebted to Warne and White *How to Hold an Audience–Without a Rope,* Chapter 3.

1. *Ask a question.* Arouse interest by asking a question for which the talk will be the answer. The introduction to a talk I have given on the crippled man let down through the roof in Mark 2:1–12 begins like this:

> "What do you think is your greatest problem? I know that is a heavy way to begin this talk but nonetheless it is important. No one is going to ask you to tell, so there is no reason why you shouldn't be honest. For some people, it will be unemployment. For others, a relationship which is falling apart. For others, it will be low self-esteem. For others, it is just not being able to get on with people. Tonight's talk is about a man who came to Jesus and had his greatest problem solved. Let me read the passage in the Bible."

2. *Use shocking statements and statistics.* Sometimes people's interest can be aroused by the shock of the opening statement. I well remember a talk I heard more than 20 years ago at St Luke's', Miranda. Peter Watson was preaching. The church was jampacked with young adults. He began the talk with: "The present statistics we have available are such that in ten year's time less than one in three of you here tonight will still be attending church at all. Please listen to this talk so that you will not be one who will fall away."

I did listen. It was a shock to me!

Care needs to be taken that the shock is not so great that people continue to think about the problem rather than the solution.

3. *Appeal to a known need.* Often when speaking to elderly people, whose health and capacities have been lessened and who may think they are unimportant, I begin

by saying, "Do you know that God thinks you are a very important person? Let me read the part of the Bible that assures us of this. I am reading John 3:16 etc."

As an introduction to the woman at the well in John 4, I begin:

> "Do you ever think that life is a drudgery? You just never seem to get on top of things. You can't remember seeing the bottom of the ironing basket since your mother-in-law last visited. The Bible tells of someone who was like this and she met Jesus and was never the same again."

4. *Tell a story.* The most common way to introduce the talk is to tell a story. Find one that raises the question or the need the talk will meet. I want to advise against using your biggest and best illustration as the introduction. In the first place we, the hearers, don't know what it is illustrating and you will have to re-activate it later. Stories re-told are never as good.

Some other suggestions

Try to keep the introduction as brief as possible. It doesn't need to be any longer than to do the things that are stated above.

Don't tell a story to illustrate the introduction. If the introduction isn't good enough without the illustration, it isn't good enough.

If you are telling a story, there is no need for two stories, unless neither of them is good enough, in which case scrap them both.

The introduction doesn't need to do more that set the scene. As soon as it is done, get to the Bible. The Bible is so good it will carry the talk along.

When you have finished this part of the talk, read it aloud and see what it 'sounds' like. See if you can make it briefer and still not lose any of the impact. Try out an alternative and see if it sounds better. Put it on tape and play it back in a couple of days and ask the question—"Would I want to listen to the rest of the talk?". If the answer is in the negative, try again. If positive, then go for it.

An opening prayer

Up to this stage, I have said nothing about an opening prayer. You should give thought as to whether the inclusion of an opening prayer is wise since the talk is basically designed for unbelievers. For some people it will be distracting, for others it will be helpful.

If you decide to pray before the talk, use it to focus people's minds on the subject at hand. Here is an example:

> "Heavenly Father, please help me to teach the Bible in such a way that we will hear you speaking to us. Please help us to respond to you in a way that pleases you."

Background material

Often people give background material to set the Bible passage in its context at the end of the introduction. However, it does not always need to be given at this point. It can be given at the point in the talk where it is needed. You can say, "I need to interrupt the story here to give you some background material". An example of this is found in Chapter 7 on page 98 and in the talk in Appendix I on page 186. Often when people give background material at the beginning, it can easily get out of hand and much more background is given than is needed. When the flow of the talk has been interrupted, you will be anxious to get back to it, so don't give any more background material than is necessary for the part of the Bible you are dealing with.

A sample introduction

Here is the introduction for the Christmas talk I have been preparing in Chapter 7. It is to be delivered at a Carol Service where there will be a lot of children as well as adults. I want it to be a 'fun' introduction. I want it to be enjoyable and playful. Here it is:

Do you remember when you were expecting your first child or when your first brother or sister was born? Do you remember the discussions about what the baby would be called? Perhaps you got one of those books with names and their meanings. If you did you would have discovered that if your name is Nigel it means Champion. If your name is Helen it means pleasant. Claire—bright. Agatha—good woman. I have a friend working in the Highlands of New Guinea. They found a tribe of natives who had heard some English words but did not know their meanings. They liked the sound of them so they called their children by these words. One man was named "Tinned fish", another "Second gear".

My father gave me the name "John." It means the gift of God. I think he may have wished to revise it as I grew up!

In the part of the Bible that I am about to read, you find that there are two names given to Jesus. If you understand the meanings of these names you will understand the true meaning of Christmas. See if you can find them as I read the passage.

Summary

1. The first words spoken should be used to arouse interest in the subject of the talk.
2. When all the necessary information has been given in the talk, conclude it thoughtfully and as quickly as possible.

CHAPTER TEN

Practising the talk

What is in this chapter?
1. What sort of notes will we need from which to speak?
2. What are the relative values of various methods?
3. It is necessary to practise the talk until its content is known by the speaker.

By this stage, you should have the talk written out. You are now faced with a decision as to what form the notes from which you will give your talk will take.

I have heard some very fine speakers who never take any notes at all with them when they speak. They have so mastered the text of the talk that it is unnecessary for them even to have a memory jog.

At the other end of the spectrum, I have heard equally good speakers who work from a complete manuscript. They have also mastered their material and I suspect they could do just as good a job without it. The manuscript acts as a sort of security blanket.

I am a speaker who works at a half-way position. I write out a manuscript and then reduce it to notes. I have preached in both of the above ways. I have even prepared without writing out any notes at all. I abandoned that method because it took me so much longer than by writing some notes. I didn't think the end result was any better than the method I had used before. I personally find working from a full manuscript very difficult indeed. This may well be because I have never done it, even when I was a beginner.

Whatever gets the best results for you is the method you should use. In the end, what matters is that the communication be clear and interesting. How this is achieved is secondary.

Everyone is personally addressed

Whatever method you use, it is important that the talk should not 'sound' as if it is read. It should be such that everyone in the audience should feel that they have been personally spoken to and this can only be achieved by looking at the people for most of the time. From the signals coming back from the audience, the speaker should know if they are listening, if they have understood, if their attention is flagging and if it is time to stop. This cannot be done if the speaker is not observing them. Looking at their eyes will give you the best feedback, as your eyes will also tell them how important you think the message is. Both need to make constant contact. I never cease to be amazed that people who have heard good speakers, think that the speakers know them, even though there might have been hundreds there listening with them!

No agreement from the specialists

Warne and White say:

> Notes destroy a great deal of audience interest. They can be a barrier between a speaker and audience. Anyone who reads the full text of an address can fall into a number of traps. The first trap is writing the address in literary rather than conversational English. When read aloud, the speech sounds stilted and unnatural.[1]

From their point of view, notes are for emergencies. The secular communicator, Peter Thompson, in his useful book on public speaking, makes a similar point. He advises speakers that although you may wish to take a full manuscript with you, simply reading it out is to be avoided.

D. Martin Lloyd–Jones will not lay down a hard and fast rule, but he is adamant that there should be a freedom in speaking and that notes or a manuscript should not restrict this freedom.[2]

I think the wisest course is for me to describe all the methods and give some pros and cons for each.

1. *Without notes or manuscript.*

This method allows the maximum freedom to speakers. They can give themselves totally to the congregation. Neither the speaker nor the listener is distracted by reference to notes. There is also freedom to spend more time or less, as the speaker perceives that something has or has not been grasped.

The difficulties with this method arise from its advan-

---

1. Warne and White, *How to Hold an Audience–Without a Rope* p 67
2. D. Martin Lloyd-Jones, *Preaching and Preachers*, pp 82–84

tages. The speaker must be disciplined time-wise and not just dribble on. Also, there is no fallback position here. If you forget what you are on about, you are on your own.

2. With full oral manuscript.

The advantages of this method are obvious. You always know what you want to say. It offers a wide variety of vocabulary. You won't always be using the same words and phrases as we are all tempted to do when we ad-lib.

The possible difficulties here are that, if the talk is read, it will be difficult for the hearers to feel that they are being spoken *with*. They may well feel that they have been spoken *to*.

If this method is used, it is essential to write the text in a speaking style and not in a writing style.

3. Speaking with notes

This method should give the best of both of the above methods. The manuscript is first written and then notes are made from it. These notes are memory 'jogs' and they should be sufficiently detailed for the speaker to function satisfactorily.

If either notes or manuscript are used, they must be written large enough for speakers to read them with ease when they are standing.

Notes should be written on paper that is not obtrusive and does not distract your listeners as the pages are turned. You would be wise to check the size of the note rack on the stand where you will be delivering the talk to see if it is big enough to carry both your notes and your Bible. If this is a problem, why not write out the Bible passages in your notes or manuscript.

If your talk is an after-dinner address, you can be fairly

certain that there will not be a stand or note rack available, and you may have to hold the microphone in one hand. I have found it helpful to have a cheap Bible into which I have glued the notes of the talk. I glue them into the margin opposite the passage on which I am speaking.

If you are using the talk more than once, you should keep the full manuscript as well as the notes from which you have spoken. This will save time when you re-prepare it for the next occasion. It is remarkable how quickly some talks go out of date, particularly the illustrations.

No substitute for knowing the talk

It is worth saying that, whatever method you use, no method is a substitute for *knowing the content of the talk thoroughly*.

If you, the speaker, after having spent ten hours preparing the talk, can't remember what is in it, then what hope is there for me, the listener, to remember it after twenty minutes?

If the speaker cannot remember the content of the talk, it is either because it is too complicated, in which case it will have to be simplified, or it has not been practised enough.

Practising the talk

When you have decided what form your talk will take, the task of practising begins.

Practise aloud so you can 'hear' what it sounds like. Practise all the time from your notes or from the manuscript you intend to take with you. During this first practice session you may discover a simpler or more powerful way to say something. Revise the notes. You may find that some words or phrases are difficult to read. This may be because of your writing or because the combination of words is difficult. Change your notes. If you stumble over some section then revise it. Abandon any idea that 'it will be better on the night'. My experience is that it is always slightly worse.

When you practise it the second time, take a note of the length of the talk. I have followed the practice of noting each five minutes with a (5), (10), (15) mark in the margin of the notes. I take a stopwatch with me so that I know where I should be after every five minutes.

It will take slightly longer when you are on your feet than it does in the study. For me to speak for twenty minutes it should take sixteen in the study.

If time is important in the program, I have found it helpful to block out sections of the talk that, in an emergency, can be left out without wrecking the logic of the talk. It is very difficult to start to revise it when you are on your feet. The decision to shorten the talk should be made before you begin.

What remains to be done now is to practise the talk over and over again until you are completely conversant with its content and its order. This is another reason why preparing early is essential. You need plenty of time to practise the talk, to gather illustrations and to work on the introduction.

In my experience, there is no substitute for this step in effective preaching. If you are taking a full manuscript with you so you will hope to by-pass this, forget it. And if at the other end of the scale you have decided to have no notes and to make it up as you go along, that will be equally disastrous for us, the hearers. Please have mercy on us and learn it yourself so that we can learn what you have to say in the most user-friendly way.

There is nothing like good preaching. It is great.

There is absolutely nothing like the opposite. It is the pits.

Sample notes

Just for interest, here is a copy of the notes I took with me for the sample talk I have been preparing with you on Matthew 1:18–23.

Title	**The True Meaning of Christmas**
Intro.	Remember the first baby.
	Book of names: Nigel = champ. Helen = pleasant. Claire = bright Agatha = good woman.
	Tinned fish, Second gear.
	The true meaning of Christmas is found in two names that are given to Jesus. See if you can spot them as I read Matthew 1:18–23.
Body	Jesus = Saviour
	Emmanuel = God with us
	Christmas is about forgiveness
	v 21 Jesus saves his people from their sins.
	What is sin and why does it matter?
	How does Jesus save us?
	Surfing rescue illustration
	Do you know what it is to be forgiven?
	Christmas is about friendship
	Because of forgiveness we can become friends with him.
	Jesus = Emmanuel = God with us = all the time.
	Do you know that?
	Tonight these could both be yours.

A compromise

A student of mine showed me a half-way house between a full manuscript and notes. He had a wide margin on the left-hand side of his manuscript and he wrote notes for preaching in this margin opposite the part in the manuscript that the note referred to. He practised from these notes and preached from them. However if he had a memory lapse or through nervousness forgot what he was on about, all he had to do was to glance over to the manuscript and start reading until be 'got back into the saddle' again.

I guess if he had been doing my talk, it would have looked like this:

Do you remember the first baby? Nigel = champion Helen = pleasant Claire = bright Agatha = good woman	**The True Meaning of Christmas** Do you remember when you were expecting your first child or when your first brother or sister was born? Do you remember the discussion about what the baby would be called? Perhaps you got one of those books with names and their meanings. If you did then you would have discovered that if your name is Nigel it means Champion! If your name is Helen it means—pleasant. Claire—bright. Agatha—good woman. I have friends working in the highlands of New Guinea. They found a tribe of natives who had heard some English words that they liked the sound of but didn't know the meaning. They liked the sound so much that they had called their children with these names. They

Tinned fish
Second Gear

found a man who was called 'Tinned fish' and another called 'Second Gear'.

John

My father gave me the name John. It means the gift of God. I think if he had known its meaning he may well have revised it in time!!

Two names of Jesus

In the part of the Bible I am about to read you will find that there are two names given to Jesus. If you understand the meaning of these names you will understand the true meaning of Christmas.

Read Matthew 1:18–23

Read Matthew 1:18 –23.

Jesus = Savior
Jesus = Emmanuel
= God with us

Did you notice the two names? The first one was in verse 21. "You shall call his name Jesus because he will save his people from their sins". The second one is in verse 23 "...Emmanuel which means God with us".

Christmas is about forgiveness

The first thing I want to draw to your attention is that:
Christmas is about forgiveness

When I say that Christmas is about forgiveness I don't mean that I should forgive you or that you should forgive me however important that might be etc.

Keep experimenting with different methods. And see which method is the most comfortable for you to handle.

Summary
1. There are different methods of speaking. Some use notes and some do not.
2. There are various ways of writing notes for use when giving a talk. You would be wise to experiment until you find a method that you can use with ease.
3. The more time you leave to practise the talk, the better it is likely to be.

CHAPTER ELEVEN

Immediate follow-up after the talk

What is in this chapter?

1. Some methods of asking for public response to the gospel have left much to be desired. There must be good reasons for doing it.
2. There are some reasons why it is helpful.
3. Some times and some methods are inappropriate.
4. There are a variety of ways that we can ask for a response.

We need to address our minds to what has been called in the past an 'appeal' or an 'altar call'. We need to work out whether there is value in doing it and, if so, what will be the most appropriate way for the group with which we are working.

Is a public response a necessary part of repentance?

Many people have suffered in the past from over-emotional appeals. In fact, the evangelistic talks of my youth seemed to have more appeal than they had content.

I remember going to a meeting one night. At the end of the talk the 'evangelist' asked everyone to stand. Then he asked all the Christians to sit down! As if that wasn't bad enough, he then asked all those who wanted to become Christians to sit. Well, who do we have left now? Why the intransigents! The evangelist thundered away until all wilted under the strain. There was a one hundred percent response! I personally thought that people must have found it hard to believe that they were loved when they had been treated so shamefully. It was pure manipulation. In 1979, I was the chairman of the Follow-Up Committee for the Sydney Billy Graham Crusade. Let me say that I am a great admirer of Billy Graham and I thought the 1979 Crusade had a large and valuable impact on Sydney and its churches. As chairman, I was given a daily copy of the statistics of people who had come out for counselling the night before. I was interested to note that by far the largest group that came out for the first time was teenagers. Almost all of the adults who responded had responded like this somewhere else when they were teenagers. It seemed clear to me that teenagers were able to ask for help in this way better than adults could, and that we needed to find a better way to help adults.

In fact, we ought to ask the question, "Do we need to do this at all?" and, if the answer is positive, "What are our reasons for doing it?".

D Martyn Lloyd–Jones in *Preaching and Preachers* gives several reasons why he thinks this is a completely inappropriate way to behave.[1]

He suggests that calling for some public act of repen-

---

1.   Chapter 14

tance as a means of 'closing the deal' is ultimately a distrust of the Holy Spirit—that we feel that something more than preaching the gospel in the power of the Spirit is required to hasten and supplement the process, and so we have an altar call to 'push people over the line'.

He argues that those who do this think that, without it, people will not turn to Christ and that this will 'help' them to make a decision which otherwise they would not make.

I must say that given the premises on which he works, I agree with him.

I have heard it argued that, in the Bible, everyone who came to Jesus did so publicly. This has been used as a justification for insisting on the need for an outward response. I do not think this argument can be sustained. I am sure that Nicodemus is an exception,[2] as is the man whose son is healed in John 4:46–54. The woman at the well in John 4 also seems to be an exception. It is true that she goes to the people and tells them about Jesus, but this was a consequence of her new recognition of Jesus as Messiah and not a part of it.

Sooner or later, all believers will have to identify themselves with Jesus as their Saviour and Lord, but immediate witness is not an essential feature of genuine repentance. Those who have worked with people who have answered appeals know that some people respond for reasons other than that they have been saved.

Whatever we do, we should take care not to allow people to believe that because they have made some public response to the message they are automatically

---

2.   Jn 3:1–8

saved. The parable of the seed in the different soils should warn us that immediate response is no guarantee of ultimate response. Those who comprise the seed sown on the rocky ground are those who "at once receive it (the word) with joy".[3] Initially they cannot be distinguished from the seed on the good ground. Both make the same outward response.

Is there a place for some public response?

1. The only reason I can see for asking for a response from people who have made a decision to follow Christ as Lord and trust him as their Saviour is to check on their understanding. This enables us to correct any errors in their understanding and to offer some instruction in the long-term implications of their decision.

Because I am convinced that the making of a public response is not an integral part of repentance, I have broken the connection between the act of repentance and faith, and the overt witness to that act. This being the case, it is important to separate an outward immediate response from praying a prayer of commitment. A good idea would be to sing a song after the talk and the prayer. This will help people to see that calling for an outward response is a different activity. This process could be further helped if the call for a response is made by the person leading the meeting, rather than the person who gave the talk. The way in which it is done should also show that we do not believe it to be part of Christian obedience.

Rather, it is an option that is offered to people who judge, for themselves, that it could be helpful to them. I

---

3. Mk 4:16

think it would be helpful but I put no pressure on them. It has nothing to do with their coming to Christ.

2.   I am also looking for a way to make contact with people who may have been affected by the preaching of the word and who, for one reason or another, have not come to Christ. I would like to enrol them in a course designed for enquirers.[4] We need a mechanism whereby such people can be contacted.

3.   It allows, in some way, for people who have turned to Christ to make a witness to that fact without having to tell everyone immediately.

For what reasons is it inappropriate?

While asking for a response is appropriate under some circumstances, let me say when and why I think it will be inappropriate.

1. To see if the gospel is working.

There is no doubt in my mind that the Holy Spirit will take the gospel we have preached and do with it, in the hearts of the hearers, what he will. I will try to persuade people by every legitimate means to respond to the gospel with repentance and faith. But telling us about your response, and asking for further help, has nothing to do with repentance and faith. If a person turns to Christ in repentance and faith, that person is truly a child of God whether they tell us or not. Telling God is what is important.

2. To see which talk works better than another.

If a speaker asks for an outward response so he or she can

---

4.   For example: M. Bennett, *Christianity Explained* (Scripture Union, 1989); J. Dickson, *Simply Christianity* (Mathias Media, 1998).

judge the effectiveness of one evangelistic talk over another, it will not be long before that speaker loses the gospel altogether. People are more likely to respond when there has been no real explanation of what is involved in following Jesus. Unless I am mistaken, that speaker will stop telling people about the judgement of God altogether, or any other truth which is not positive. The gospel is indeed good news if we respond positively to it and its demands. It is very bad news if we reject it. If results are the work of the Holy Spirit, and they are,[5] then how people react to the gospel on a given day is his department. As I have mentioned, the parable of the soils should warn us that an initial response to the gospel may have very little to do with the ultimate response.[6] The effectiveness of the gospel, from our point of view, lies in the accuracy and urgency with which we preach it and not in the immediate response that people make to it.

3. To justify our preaching.

We should not ask people to tell us that they have turned to Christ so that we can justify ourselves as evangelists either to ourselves, or to the Christian community, or to God himself. I wouldn't mention this were it not for the fact that so many promotional videos of evangelists spend a lot of time showing people coming out to be counselled. It is unfortunately true that I can hardly ever make a judgement on the effectiveness of the preaching by watching the videos. This must be an attempt to show that they really are good at their job. If you discover that you are

---

5. See 2 Cor 4:6
6. Mk 4:1–20

doing it for this reason you probably would be wise to stop using whatever method you are currently using.

4. So we can publish the statistics.

The very last reason we should make an appeal is so that we can tell people how wonderful it all was and how many people came to Christ. This behaviour is so inappropriate because it shows that our confidence is not on the God who works by his word but on the immediate response.

May I remind you of how bad the statistics of the Lord Jesus' campaign in Korazin, Bethsaida and Capernaum were? Here we have the best speaker who ever was. He was the finest of miracle workers and, in spite of the fact that he had performed most of his miracles in these cities, no-one repented. You can read it for yourself in Matthew 11:20–30. It is salutary to note the reason that the Lord Jesus gives for this lack of response in verses 25 and 26:

> I praise you, Father, Lord of heaven and earth, because **you have hidden these things from the wise and learned, and revealed them to little children. Yes, Father, for this was your good pleasure.**

It had nothing to do with the effectiveness of his preaching.

What will we do?

We are looking for a mechanism that will enable people who want help to ask for it. This will vary from place to place and with the size of the group that has been listening to us. Thought needs to be given as to what would be the most appropriate way to do this.

1. Make a phone call.

If you are the minister or pastor of the church, and the congregation is not a large one, it may not need more than for you to say something like this: "If today has been a turning point for you, we should meet as soon as possible and talk about it. If you phone me this afternoon we could make an appointment. My phone number is on the program you were given when you came in." If this method is used, it is important for the person who has issued the invitation to be in that afternoon and answer the phone. Don't expect them to leave their details on the answering machine!

2. Ask people to wait behind.

People who have responded can be asked to stay in their places as others leave and their names and addresses can be taken or some immediate instruction can be given. They can be given literature explaining what they have done and the immediate way forward. This procedure is inappropriate where I go to church because people do not leave the building but stay and talk. If your church is like this, you may be able to find a quiet place where you will not be disturbed. It would be wise to speak with them where everyone can see what is going on so there can be no suspicion of any wrong doing. I sometimes suggest that they might like to come with a friend.

3. Ask for a booklet or a video.

People can be directed to introduce themselves to an identified person, and to ask for some literature or a video that will help them.

4. Fill in a comment card.

People can be asked to fill in a comment card that enables them to ask for help. Here is a sample one:

Confidential

Name..

Address...

....

..........................Post code................

Phone..

☐ Prayed

☐ More

☐ Enjoyed

Comments...

....

....

....

....

When using such a card I explain its purpose in the following way:

> "We, at this church, are anxious that people should get the best **help** that we can give them in becoming a Christian and growing up strong in the Christian life.
>
> "You may have made a new beginning and

prayed the prayer with me. If you did this and meant it, you can be sure that your prayer has been heard and that God will indeed forgive you. Welcome to God's people. You have begun a new life with Christ. New people need help and the only way that we can get help to you is for you to ask us. We have devised a simple way for you to do that.

"When you came here today you were given a card which is marked **Confidential.** Will you please get that out now. I am going to ask everyone if they would fill it in.

"If you prayed along with me and you would like help, put an X in the 'Prayed' box and we will get help to you.

"You may not have done this, but today has shown you that you need to investigate Christianity further. If we can help you, put an X in the 'More' box and we will phone you and inform you about what we are offering for people who want more information.

"You may not want to take either of these options. The 'Enjoyed' box is so you won't feel out of it. If you would like to make a comment please do so.

"If you are asking for help we will need to know who you are and how we can contact you. Let me stress that this information will be treated with confidence. The Minister will see them and arrange help to get to you."

If you use this method please note:
a)   You need to have enough cards and pencils for everyone.
b)   Please explain to people *why* you are asking them to fill in the card before you ask them to

do it. Assure them that they will not receive mailing or be contacted unless they ask for it.

c) Tell them who will see the card and stress the *confidential* nature of the exercise.

d) Explain what will happen if they fill it in.

e) Explain where they should put the card when it is completed.

This method enables us to find the interested people who have not as yet become Christians and to get help to the ones who have.

5. Ask for a copy of the prayer.

A friend of mine organises evangelistic dinners for business people. They meet at a function room, with tables seating eight people. Tickets are sold to Christian business people in sets of eight, and people are encouraged to bring a table of guests. At the end of the talk, a prayer is prayed for people to receive Christ like the one I used in Chapter 9. After that, the chairperson says, "If you prayed along tonight you may like a copy of the prayer. We have them printed on a card that you could put into your wallet or purse. If you indicate to your host he or she will come and get one for you."

The host will know who should be followed up by this simple method.

6. The clipboard at the bookstall.

Depending on the group and its size, you may not need to do anything more than to say something like this:

> "If tonight was an important night for you and we can help you, you will find a clipboard on the Bookstall. If you put your name and address on it

we will contact you and arrange a time to meet."

I have mentioned the methods used by other people to show that there are any number of ways we can offer help. It is up to you to think about the one that you will be happy using and that you judge the group will be happy to respond to.

I don't tell people that they will be 'counselled' or that 'counsellors' will be available. It sounds like professional counselling of some kind. Just tell them that someone will help them.

Plan carefully
Whatever method is used, it is important to plan carefully what is to happen. The 'instructions' should be scripted so that the explanation does not take on a life of its own and become the talk after the talk.

Check with the organisers
If you are a visitor at the church or group where you have been invited to speak, check with the organisers before you make a decision about whether this sort of response would be appropriate and what method they think is most suitable for them. Remember, they have to live with the group after you have left!

Summary
1. Making some public response (like going forward) is not an integral part of repentance.
2. We are looking for ways to help people that are appropriate for their needs and make it easy for them to ask for help.
3. Such methods may differ in differing situations.

CHAPTER TWELVE

Choosing the right kind of talk and the right length

What is in this chapter?

1. It is not possible to say everything in the Bible in one talk.
2. How will we work out what must be said and what can be left out?

Do we have to say it all?

A man once asked me if I could explain the gospel to him in three minutes. I said I thought I could. "Well why do you persist in spending twenty-five minutes doing it?" he replied.

Good question!

When the Philippian jailer asks the apostle Paul what he has to do to be saved, the answer is short and clear. "Believe in the Lord Jesus, and you will be saved—you and your household."[1]

The gospel in a sentence. But what a sentence! It is

---

1. Acts 16:31

totally loaded. No doubt that is why we are told that they then "spoke the word of the Lord to him and to all the others in his house".[2] They needed to explain what the sentence meant. It wasn't because it was inadequate. It was because it was so concentrated in its meaning. Its implications needed to be spelt out.

If at one end of the spectrum we have the gospel in a sentence, at the other end we have the overall message of the Bible. It is also the gospel. It will make us "wise for salvation through faith in Jesus Christ".[3]

Mark begins his story about Jesus with the words: "The beginning of the gospel about Jesus Christ, the Son of God."[4] Presumably he thinks his book is the gospel.

There is no doubt that John thinks that his Gospel is a statement of the gospel because he tells us the purpose of the Gospel. "These things are written that you may believe that Jesus is the Christ, the Son of God, and that by believing you may have life in his name."[5]

I suppose when we are preaching the gospel in a talk, which might take twenty minutes, we are about mid-way on the spectrum. To do this, some selection of available material must be made. We cannot say everything in the time we have.

Avoid overload

When reading Peter Thompson's *Persuading Aristotle*, I came across this quote:

---

2. Acts 16:32
3. 2 Tim 3:15
4. Mk 1:1
5. Jn 20:31

> To avoid overloading your audience with informa-
> tion, you must be absolutely clear about your
> message. It is a common mistake for speakers to
> show people far more information than is neces-
> sary to support the point they are making.[6]

It was painful to read it. It brought back a memory that I
would rather have left forgotten. Soon after I had learned
to use *2 Ways to Live*,[7] I thought that I would preach it
as a sermon. You will recall that this method of telling
people the gospel is accompanied with a set of six draw-
ings that illustrate six different statements of theology.
There is also a verse from the Bible with each drawing to
further illustrate the truth being taught. The fact that
there were six verses from the Bible should have been a
warning bell clanging in my ears that there would be far
too much material for one talk. There is no fool like an
old fool. However, it is such a good gospel statement that
I found it irresistible. It begins with creation and proceeds
to the Fall, to judgement, the atonement, the resurrection
of the Lord Jesus, and the need for repentance and faith.
Surely I couldn't fail with such a wonderful recipe!

It was a disaster. I had a large white board on which I
proceeded to do the illustrations as I explained the gospel.
It took fifty minutes. Tidal wave after tidal wave of information swept over the unsuspecting audience. It is a
measure of the long-suffering nature of this church, Christ
Church, Gladesville, that they have invited me back again.

---

6.   Peter Thompson, *Persuading Aristotle*, p 105
7.   If you are unfamiliar with this gospel outline, it is published by
Matthias Media. I have also described it my *Know and Tell the
Gospel* (Matthias Media, 1998) pp 156–161.

I certainly didn't deserve it. To add insult to injury, the following day I met a friend, Peter Watson, who told me that he had decided to give a six-week series of talks using *2 Ways to Live* as the basis. He gave one talk on each of the major themes. I don't doubt they were excellent.

On reflection, I think that it could have been done if I hadn't insisted on giving all the propositions equal time and emphasis. I have heard Phillip Jensen use the outline on several occasions at University missions very effectively. He has majored on one of the propositions and has mentioned the others almost in passing.

How much information do we need?
I have already drawn your attention to the way the apostle Paul described the model response of the Thessalonians. What information were they given that enabled them to respond like this?

> They turned to God from idols to serve the living and true God and to wait for his Son from heaven, whom he raised from the dead—Jesus who rescues us from the coming wrath.[8]

We know from Acts 17 that Paul spoke at their synagogue on three successive Sabbaths. He may well have spoken privately to people in between times. In the Jewish synagogue he could have assumed a fair degree of knowledge of the Old Testament Scriptures. In fact, we know that he showed from the Scriptures how Jesus had to suffer, die and rise again from the dead.[9]

---

8. 1 Thess 1:9–10
9. Acts 17:3

There is no doubt that the person and work of the Lord Jesus must have been dealt with carefully, including his sin-bearing death and his return as judge. Instruction must also have been given about the uniqueness of God and of his desire to be served.

The Bible offers variety

One of the wonders of the Bible is its ability to say the same truths over and over again in so many different ways. It does this with propositional statements, with stories, sometimes in poetry, sometimes in prose. It offers a wide variety of material for gospel ministry. However, as we read the Bible, we discover that some parts emphasise a particular aspect of the truth more than another. It is important to take this on board so we don't feel guilty about not saying everything every time

Different stories—different truths

Certain parts of the Bible will emphasise different truths. If we expound them carefully, we will always be fresh in our approach and not predictable.

An example of this can be seen in the story of the 'sinful' woman in Luke 7:36-50. This story has as its main theme forgiveness and loving God.[10] What will be emphasised will be the nature of sin and the wonder of forgiveness. While the death of the Lord Jesus will be mentioned, it will not have the same attention as the other truths.

The story of the woman at the well in John 4:42 will have as its main thrust that the Lord Jesus can fill the emptiness and loneliness that is experienced by the alter-

---

10. You can read a talk on this passage in Appendix 1 on p 183.

native to him.

The rich fool in Luke 12 is a direct challenge to those who are materialists and are not rich towards God.

A talk on 1 Thessalonians 1:9–10 will deal with repentance and faith as its major theme.

When preaching on the statement in Mark 10:45— "For even the Son of Man did not come to be served, but to serve, and give his life as a ransom for many"—the greater bulk of time will be spent on the nature of the substitutionary death of the Lord Jesus on our behalf. Mention would be made of the kingdom of God and that Jesus is its king but this would be a minor point compared with the main thrust of the death of the Lord Jesus.

I have included several talks in Appendices I–IV. You will see how different talks vary in the major treatment given to different truths.

However, if we choose to leave out certain truths because we think they will be unpalatable to the hearer (e.g. God's judgement) then this is not good enough.

What if the cross isn't in the passage?

Given the importance of the death and resurrection of the Lord Jesus Christ, I always make mention of it whether it is in the passage I am dealing with or not. I may introduce it by saying, "What we know is that they, as yet, did not know that Jesus' death is the means whereby we can be forgiven. There was no way they could know this before it had happened. We, on the other hand, are very fortunate to live now and know it for ourselves."

Sometimes I introduce it by saying, "Before this book finishes, we know that Jesus died in our place taking the punishment our sins deserve...".

It has been suggested that in the sermons recorded in the

Acts of the Apostles, the death of Jesus for the forgiveness of sins (the atonement) is hardly mentioned. This is true. However, the following points are worth thinking about:

1. The Apostle Paul tells us the gospel he preached to the Corinthians (1 Cor 15:1-8).

2. We have only a summary of what was said in the sermons in Acts.

3. Sometimes the atonement is not specifically mentioned, but it must have been preached.[11]

4. I am not convinced that the talks in Acts are recorded so they can be a model for our preaching, either in form or in content.

5. The resurrection of the Lord Jesus is never absent. How could that have been preached without reference to the efficacy of his sin-bearing death?

Will the material be appropriate for the audience?

We will be more engaging as gospel speakers if we stand in the shoes of those who are listening to us. What are they like? What are their fears and hopes? This will allow us to chose parts of the Bible that will scratch where they are itching. Some examples of this could be:

- John 3:16 gives us the key verse in prose for people overwhelmed with the need to know that God loves them.

- Jeremiah 31:31-34 gives reassurance for those overwhelmed by sin and guilt.

- 1 Thessalonians 1:9-10 is for those who are fearful of death and judgement.

---

11. Acts 10:42 (did Peter tell Cornelius and his household about judgement but not how to get ready?); 13:39; 17:3

- Romans 5:6-7 would do a power of good to those with low self-esteem and the need to know that God loves them.
- Luke 18:9-14 pulls the rug out from those who think that good works will justify them before God.

There is enough material in the Bible for a lifetime of gospel preaching.

Appropriate material

Since there is such a wide variety of material available, we should give careful thought to selecting passages that will be appropriate for the particular audience.

I was recently asked to preach at a jazz festival. I reckoned that most people would have come to hear the jazz singers and the bands, more than to hear the gospel. I tried to strike a note that I thought would be unexpected. I guessed that most people think of God as a sort of a policeman and against fun. I decided that the talk would be a 'fun' talk. So I chose to preach on the text from 1 Timothy 6:17—"Put your trust in the God who gives us all things richly to enjoy". I spoke about the world God created for us to enjoy. Friends for us to love and to love us. Music to enjoy. I spoke of how we didn't always enjoy life in the way God intended because of sin and how Jesus gave himself on the cross so we could be forgiven and enjoy God forever. The outline of this talk is on pages 226 and 227.

Summary

Since we are unable to say everything every time, we should select passages that give people sufficient information to make the response we are asking from them.

CHAPTER THIRTEEN

Some general comments: nuts and bolts

What is in this chapter?

This chapter is a series of tips on giving talks. They don't bear much relationship to each other but they are worth knowing.

Different styles—different books

You don't have to read the Bible for very long before you discover that different parts of it are written in different styles. Some of the Bible stories are history, like the Gospels and 1 and 2 Samuel. Others are poetry, like the Psalms and Proverbs. Others are straight teaching like Romans and Ephesians. Still others are a combination of all of these, like Isaiah.

It is important to have the style of a particular book in our minds when we are preaching from it. We should not reduce all Scripture into propositional forms and apply the formula I have suggested in Chapters 6–13.

When the part of the Bible is a story, try not to destroy the story by saying something like, "There are three things we learn from this story", and proceed as if it had come from the epistle to the Romans. When it is a story, we want it to sound like a story.

The talk needs to have form, nonetheless. I often do that by saying: "This story comes to us in three scenes", or "This story is about three people and we are going to look at each one in turn", and so on.[1]

If the talk we are giving is from poetry, we can say something like, "Do you see what the poet is doing here? There are three major movements", or "Did you notice how the poet felt about this issue?". As you express yourself, try to be more 'poetic' in your choice of words and expressions.

Exceptions to the rules

Every now and again, you will hear someone preach who is quite exceptional and who, at the same time, seems to break all the rules about good preaching. Don't let this throw you. It is because they are exceptional that they get away with it. I can think of three of my friends who are very fine speakers. They are exceptionally clever, and so are always interesting to listen to. They are gifted communicators, and so are always easy to listen to. This is a winning combination. They are outstanding and we would all like to be able to preach like them.

However, people like this are the exceptions. Others who try to be like them are often failures. We see and hear them at the height of their powers and they are very experienced. They did not preach like they do now when they were beginners. If you are a beginner, please preach with form and structure and become proficient in one method before you start experimenting. Because they are excep-

---

1. See Appendix I.

tions, they can often preach for longer than we can. You might become a speaker like them in time but, in the meantime, stick to the method I have suggested and you will get better-than-average results, and faster, than if you don't.

Learning by listening to others
Often we learn more about preaching by listening to good models than we do by reading a book about it. This is a great age where we are able to listen, on tape, and now even on the internet, to the best speakers in the world and at our leisure.

Learning by listening to yourself
While I am talking about tapes, let me say that I believe it is a good idea to listen to your own talks on tape. If you don't, you will be the only person who engages in audio communication but never listens to the communication. How can we know what we sound like if we never listen to ourselves? If you are a beginner, you will be a better listener to talks than you are a speaker, simply because you will have had so much more practice.

I have found that if I listen to a talk immediately after I have just given it, it always seems good. If I put it away for a few days and then listen, it never seems as good as I thought it was on the day I gave it. Initially, I think I am too close to it. I hear myself saying things that in fact were not said at all. My experience with the students I teach is that they will pick up 90% of the corrections if, after a few days, they listen to themselves.

Time in preparation
Many things we do are personal. The amount of time taken to prepare a talk will vary from person to person

and sometimes from time to time. Sometimes you can get everything down very quickly and at other times you feel as if you are walking through porridge. For me, it generally takes about eight hours at the desk for half an hour on my feet. However, the preparation period really is much longer than this. Because I do a couple of hours preparation a day, this leaves a lot of time from one day to the next to think about it and to mull it over in my mind. I can't remember ever sitting down at the desk and working from beginning to end on a talk. However, I do have as many as three talks being prepared at the same time.

About half the time in preparation is devoted to studying the Bible passage and reading commentaries. The other half is used for packaging the talk. Of this half, half of it is used on preparing the introduction. This is strange in a way because it takes up such a short amount of time in the talk. However, if I can get people's attention and stimulate them to want to hear what the Bible has to say, then this is time well spent. Once I get them into the Bible, I know it will carry them along with its content. It is getting them there and causing them to want to listen that is hard work.

Length of time in speaking

Most people who sit and listen to talks are agreed that speakers speak for too long. You *may* be the exception I was speaking about earlier in this chapter, but my advice is to assume you are not. The ideal length of time for a talk is when people say, "I could have listened to that person for another hour". If anyone ever says that to you, you will know that you finished at exactly the right time. If ever someone says to you, "I wish you had kept on going" thank him or her but do not take their advice! Had you, in fact, done what they suggested they would *not* have spoken to you in this way!

I know that the length of time taken to give a talk varies from culture to culture and from place to place. You may be speaking to a congregation that is able to stay with you longer than another. However, when you have finished your preparation, look over it and ask if it could be said in a shorter time. "Is there a simpler way to express this?" If there is, then do it.

Remember that if the people you're addressing are predominantly 'outsiders', they will not have heard anyone speak for more than about five minutes at a time. I note, with interest, that the leaders of most political parties in Australia have abandoned giving the long policy speeches at campaign launches that they did when I was a youth. Their minders know that most people will just not listen to them for an extended period of time. If you are preaching at a wedding and you have been asked to preach evangelistically, remember that the people to whom you are speaking are not used to listening to people speak for any length of time. See if you could do it in eight to ten minutes. Anzac Day (or Remembrance Day) would be an occasion where I would try to be brief. Carols in the park also calls for brevity, because in the open air there are so many distractions.

If you are a regular speaker, why not try to clip off five minutes one Sunday and see what the reaction from the congregation is!

In a regular congregation, I try to preach for twenty minutes.

Lighting, sound, people and your throat

All of these need your attention. Try not to stand where you have a bright light behind you, whether the lighting is natural or artificial. It is trying for the audience and it means that they will not be able to see your facial features and your eyes, both of which are helping in the communication. I don't like to speak when there is a spotlight on me and the audience is in darkness. I want to be able to see their faces to guage whether they can understand what I am saying and to pick up any other signals they wish to send me. I cannot do this if they are in the dark. Most organisers, who are not themselves speakers, often don't think about the organisation of the room from this point of view. You should speak to them about this. The audience needs to be where they can see you easily. It is also unwise to have people sitting behind you where everyone can see them. It is fatal if one of them falls asleep! It is a good idea to have everyone seated in front of you.

As well as being seen, you need, above all, to be heard. There may, or may not, be a public address system. If there is, you would be well advised to get there early and have a voice check with the person in charge. You need to be heard right to the back row. You want people seated there to hear as well as everywhere else. You may need to project your voice. It is a good idea to have a friend sit in the back row and tell you whether you are being heard clearly.

If there is a PA system, you have no control over the volume. That is why you need to get it right before you start. If the microphone needs to be adjusted to your height, quietly ask the chairperson to do that before you start speaking. Don't start by fumbling about with it. If the microphone you are to speak from is not used by anyone before you, see to the adjustment before the meeting begins.

You may find that your throat becomes dry as you are speaking. You would be advised before you start to have a glass of water and to take a sip from it. We don't know exactly why this helps, but it does. A good time to do that, after you have begun, is when you have paused to let people think or when you have asked them to look at a particular passage of the Bible and you are waiting for them to do that. Do not do it in the middle of a sentence. Try not to keep clearing your throat. Remember, swallow before you bark.

If you are giving an after-dinner address, you may be wise to remember that drinking alcohol before you speak dries your throat.

The speaker as a person

It goes without saying that the speaker must be converted. We need to know, through our own experience, what it is to have been a sinner in rebellion towards God. Through the work of the Holy Spirit, we must have come to the point where we recognise that we are rightly under the judgement of God. We must also have come to believe that the death of the Lord Jesus was for us, that he took the punishment which our sins deserved when he died on the cross.

The ministry of the Holy Spirit in us will have caused us to put our trust in the death of Jesus for our total forgiveness. We acknowledge that he has given us repentance and faith. This enables us to be right with God and at the same time to walk humbly before God and our fellow humans. We know it was God who did this for us and we seek to be obedient out of love and thankfulness to him for his great kindness. It is important for us to remember this because we are speaking from the word of God with first-hand experience. We should be confident that the God, who did this for us, through the ministry of the word, will do it for others, through the ministry of the same word, even if we are the speakers.

Temptations of speakers

What are the particular temptations that are common to evangelistic speakers? What do we specially need to take care about? For me, *pride* and *doubt* are at the top of my list. At the beginning of my ministry, I was not in the habit of being told that I was good. As time went by, this changed. Well-meaning people, who no doubt wanted to encourage me, began to tell me how helpful this had been to them and to their friends. People began to tell me that they had come to Christ by listening to talks I had given. Both of these things pleased me. I had worked hard at understanding the Bible and I had worked hard at trying to explain it carefully. It was right to be thankful to God that he had enabled me to do this. My temptation was to start to think that I had done it without his help (or not much anyway).

Pride

What should we do to prevent being eaten up with pride? I don't think we ought to play games with ourselves and pretend that what has happened was no good at all. We should be thankful to God who enabled us to do it. I try to spend time praying about this as I drive home in the car. I describe the work of the evangelist as being like someone who runs around the orchard giving the trees a shake. If the fruit is ripe, it will generally fall off. If there is no ripe fruit, then it doesn't much matter how hard you shake, no fruit will fall. On the other hand, when the fruit is really ripe, sometimes it will drop off when a cow or an old horse walks by! This has helped me not to think more highly of myself than I ought.

It is worth reminding ourselves that most people are brought to evangelistic meetings by their friends. These friends have invested a lot of their prayer life on behalf of those whom they have brought. They have also been witnessing to them, and will do so after we have finished speaking with them. The congregation has been at prayer for us, as have other friends of theirs and ours. It is a team effort. I find it helpful to remind myself that without the Holy Spirit there would be no speaker, no gospel and no talk.

Doubt

Doubt is also a particular temptation of mine. I am fearful that people will think I am foolish for believing what I do, and that nothing will happen as a result of my preaching. This is a direct assault from the Evil One. It is an irrational temptation, but it is real nonetheless. It often comes to me while I am preaching. I need to deal with it by rejecting it and asking God to help me, and to get on with the talk.

Inattention

If for some reason, you notice the congregation didn't hear or understand something you have said, then say it again, or say it differently. A car outside or a crying child may have disturbed them. Don't go on as if nothing has happened. Go over it again after the disturbance has gone away.

Post-talk syndrome

The speaker is totally absorbed with the act of speaking. For me, I find it tiring. Because there is always an adrenaline flow while I am at it, I am generally let down afterwards. I need to be able to relax, which for me is to watch TV. This is even more so after I have given a series of talks one after the other. Because I am excited at the end of most talks I have given, I often react badly to immediate criticism. I need to be especially on guard then. I ask people if I can get back to them on the matter and I ask for their phone number. I need to remind myself that most of those who are critical are on my side anyway. They might be right. If they are, the sooner I change the better. If they aren't, it doesn't hurt me to re-think it.

Summary
Remember, in preaching, the first fifty years are the hardest!

CHAPTER FOURTEEN

Speaking with passion

What is in this chapter?

1. Speakers should show by their concern and passion how important it is for their hearers to respond to the gospel. They should not present material in a detached way.
2. How can this be achieved?

A gospel to be passionate about

The American philosopher Ralph Waldo Emerson once remarked that one person with a belief is worth 99 who have only opinions. Communicator Peter Thompson (who cites this) goes on to say that he is often asked by public servants, in seminars he conducts, how they can become passionate about presenting a routine report.[1] Thankfully that it not our problem. If you are not passionate about the gospel something is really wrong. If you are

---

1. Peter Thompson, *Persuading Aristotle*.

not overwhelmed by the love of God in sending his Son to die so you can be forgiven, you are made of tougher stuff than I am. If you are not horrified by the prospect that people will spend eternity in Hell separated from God, and their loved ones, there is something amiss. It is a message to be passionate about.

And yet? It is sadly possible that sometimes speakers of the gospel sound almost clinical. It should not be.

We are part of the action

Giving gospel-oriented talks is not like delivering a lecture where we might be able to be detached from the process. We are part of the action. The message has changed our lives. We are living proof that the gospel works. We have known the experience of the hymn writer who said:

> I once was lost but now am found
> Was blind but now I see.[2]

We, who were once far off, have been brought near by the blood of Christ.[3] This should be apparent by what we say and the way we say it.

This aspect of gospelling is very important.

I think that some of us, in a sincere effort not to be manipulative and to play on people's emotions, have sometimes gone too far in the opposite direction. We end up conveying the impression that we are indifferent to the response people should make to our preaching. Perhaps we believe that if we state a proposition clearly we will not need to persuade people to believe it.

---

2. *John Newton in his hymn Amazing Grace.*
3. Eph 2:13

How can we redress this tendency? The answer is by reflecting on the gospel we are preaching and the God who first spoke the gospel to us.

The gospel matters

We don't have a tape of the Apostles, so we don't know how they sounded, but listen to the verbs they use to describe their way of speaking. They *begged* people to be reconciled to God.[4] They didn't tell, or inform, or suggest, or even advise. They begged! It is hard to do that in a detached way. They argued, reasoned, and persuaded, sometimes with tears.[5] It was a matter of life and death.

1. Use of words and phrases.

The apostles used emotive language to describe how they felt. Listen to this statement:

> I speak the truth in Christ–I am not lying, my conscience confirms it in the Holy Spirit–I have great sorrow and unceasing anguish in my heart. For I could wish that I myself were cursed and cut off from Christ for the sake of my brothers, those of my own race, the people of Israel.[6]

Or this uncontrollable outburst:

> Oh, the depth of the riches of the wisdom and knowledge of God! How unsearchable his judgements, and his paths beyond tracing out![7]

---

4. 2 Cor 5:11, 20
5. Acts 20:19
6. Rom 9:1–4
7. Rom 11:33

Or this:

> Praise be to the God and Father of our Lord Jesus
> Christ, who has blessed us in the heavenly realms
> with every spiritual blessing in Christ.[8]

What they had to say mattered to them, and they said so.

If you are the sort of person who doesn't readily express yourself in this way, you may need to build in words and phrases to help. Phrases such as "This is a really important matter", "This matter is urgent" and "Please don't miss this" could make a difference.

Ultimately this is a spiritual matter and you should pray that God will cause you to be filled with the wonder of what Christ has done for you and to help you express it with words.

Repeating the same phrase with slight variation can be powerful.

Phillip Jensen spoke passionately at the Church Missionary Society's Summer School in 1998. He was speaking about the prayer of the Lord Jesus in the garden of Gethsemane prior to his crucifixion (recorded in Mark 14:32-42). Phillip had made the point that there was no other way that forgiveness could come to us except that Jesus 'drink the cup' of God's wrath on our behalf. He was passionate and I was totally engaged. I tried, for a moment, to detach myself from the content and ask the question, "How has he achieved that?". I found it hard to do because I was so engrossed in the content. Having a tape was easier. I stopped it and rewound it. If you read this excerpt aloud you will get the feel of it better:

---

8. Eph 1:3

How blasphemous it is when we think that sin doesn't matter, that it is unimportant.

How blasphemous it is when I think that my sin is trivial—it doesn't matter!

How blasphemous it is when we think that God won't care about our sins!

How blasphemous it is when we think we are good enough for God!

What a terrible travesty of the truth—

What an appalling perversion and blasphemy it is when people think there is some other way to the Father than by the Lord Jesus Christ, and by his death on our behalf—because he cried out "If there is any other way"—and would not the Father have given him another way? There was no other way! The Cup could not be removed by anybody else but by him—and by no other means than him drinking it to the bottom. There is no other name by which we can be saved than by the name of the Lord Jesus Christ. There is no other gospel that we can preach than Christ and him crucified—because there is no possible other way than by him drinking the cup—by "the hour" coming to him.[9]

Did you notice the power of the recurring phrases and the vivid word pictures that were used? We were not left in the faintest shadow of a doubt but that *this mattered* to the speaker.

When you hear someone who is really good and you are totally engaged by him or her, see if you can detach yourself momentarily and analyse how they have managed

---

9. Phillip Jensen, *The Jesus Prayer* Mark 14:32–42, CMS Summer School 1998 Tape 4

to capture and keep your attention. When we are listening to poor speaking we can easily analyse it because we are bored out of our brains. We are glad to do anything except listen. When we are listening to good speaking it never occurs to do the exercise because we are seduced by the content. See if you can train yourself to be an objective participant. Then you can have the best of both worlds.

2. Emotion in the speaker.

There is no place for detached indifference on the part of the speaker. Paul reminds the Philippians, "I have often told you before and now say again even with tears, many live as enemies of the cross of Christ".[10] I am not talking about some 'fake' emotion that will easily be seen through, but an appropriate reaction to what we are teaching.

3. Body language.

As well as using graphic words and phrases to show the importance of what we are saying, the way we say it and the body language we use also matters.

> In his lectures on rhetoric at the Lyceum, Aristotle taught effective delivery as a key dimension of the art of persuasion. It is not just what you say, but how you say it that counts. Delivery was about a speaker's non-verbal communication: voice and body language. No matter how good your content is, if the message contained in your voice and body language doesn't fit the words you are saying, no-one will be convinced. If you don't feel committed to what you say, you can't expect others to. For example, the

---

10. Phil 3:18

speaker who delivers the opening line 'I am really happy to be here today', but who looks like they would prefer to be anywhere else in the world is certainly not sending the message in their words.[11]

To emphasise this point, Thompson goes on to cite the trial of Lindy Chamberlain. She was accused of murdering her baby. Most people were shaken by her appearance in court. She was so calm and appeared to be disassociated from what was happening. She was switched off. Why wasn't she more emotionally involved in the death of her baby? They judged that she must be guilty. She was in fact not guilty.

Everything should be 'saying' the same thing. Head, eyes, hands, body, voice and gesture should all be in tune with the words. When this is not the case we, the listeners, are confused as to which part to believe.

Warne and White suggest six different ways in which hand gestures can be used to advantage:

1. To point in directions to indicate time or place.
2. To show approval with upturned palms (as in receiving a gift).
3. To show disapproval by pushing away.
4. To distinguish between ideas by using different hands for different ideas.
5. To describe sizes and shapes.
6. To emphasise with the clenched fist, the pointing finger or the sweeping gesture.[12]

---

11. Peter Thompson, *Persuading Aristotle*, p 118
12. Warne and White, *How to Hold an Audience–Without a Rope*, pp 58–621

If it is possible to have your talk recorded on video, this will enable you to 'see' what your body language is like and the helpfulness or otherwise of your gestures. I am informed that if you are nervous, any idiosyncrasies show up in the first five minutes. It would be good to know what you are doing with your hands and face while you are speaking.

Trust me, *it really does matter*.

The gospel is serious

If you ask the question, "Why does it matter?" the answer is "Because it is serious!". The eternal destiny of the people who are listening is at stake. The Lord Jesus says, "Whoever believes in me will have eternal life".[13]

Can you remember the day you turned to Christ? In my case, I remember it well—although it was more than fifty years ago. I had reached the stage where I knew I was a sinner. I also knew that I was rightly under the judgement of God. I heard the gospel preached by a man as far removed from me in age as I am from that day. It didn't matter. I heard the voice of the living God address me. "Come unto me all you who are weary and burdened and I will give you rest".[14] It could not have been clearer if the heavens had opened and the voice of God was directly audible. What a relief it was that I could stop struggling to make myself good enough for God. It had been so frustrating. What joy it was to hear that the Lord Jesus had done it all when he died for me. Even today the 'magic' of the wonder that God wanted me and, what's more, that

---

13. See eg. Jn 3:36 and 6:47
14. Matt 11:28

he had given me the desire to want him, has not worn thin. Gospelling *is a serious matter.*

When I had finished writing *A Fresh Start,* I asked a friend to read the manuscript for me. He phoned me and said, "The chapter on 'How to become a Christian' is so severe that no one will ever want to be one".

I re-read what I had written. In my desire to make sure that I told people to count the cost of what was involved in turning to Christ, I had forgotten to tell them how good it was. I recast the chapter and started by telling all the reasons why I thought becoming a Christian was good. It was a right correction to make. If you have been preaching the gospel for a long time, it could be possible that you have fallen into my mistake. You may just have forgotten how good it is. Take time out to re-think it. Remember it again before the next occasion on which you preach the gospel and see if it makes a difference.

Gospelling is a serious matter because Heaven and Hell are realities and people are destined for one or the other. We may wish it was otherwise but it isn't. It is often hard to believe that our nice, kind, gentle, generous friends are destined for Hell unless they are saved by the grace of God. *It is a serious matter.*

The gospel is urgent

At no stage should we give the impression, either by word or attitude, that there is plenty of time and that a person may turn to Christ whenever they feel like it. God says, "Today if you hear my voice do not harden you heart".[15]

None of us knows when Christ will return. None of

---

15. Ps 95:7–8

us knows when we will die.[16] If people continue to harden their hearts against the word of God, they may find themselves unable to repent. Each time we say 'no' it is easier to keep saying it and we build up a protective layer.

Gospelling *is urgent.*

These attitudes come from being completely convinced of the truthfulness of what we are saying, of the power of the gospel to change lives, and of trusting the Holy Spirit to change people through the preaching of that gospel. I am not talking about psyching ourselves up. But I am talking about believing what we are saying and sounding as if we do.

Loving people

Loving people will help us to do everything we can to help them understand the gospel and its implications. There is no substitute for love and, when it is genuine, it is very hard to hide.

Richard Cecil said, "To love to preach is one thing; to love those to whom we preach is quite another".[17]

A good model

I have been struck again and again by the attitude of the Apostle Paul as he reminds the Thessalonians of his behaviour when he was with them. He says:

> ...our gospel came to you not simply with words, but also with power, with the Holy Spirit and with deep conviction. You know how we lived among you for your sake.[18]

---

16. Ps 139:161
17. D. Martyn Lloyd–Jones, *Preaching and Preachers*, p 92
18. 1 Thess 1:5

For the appeal we make does not spring from error or impure motives, nor are we trying to trick you. On the contrary, we speak as men approved by God to be entrusted with the gospel. We are not trying to please men but God, who tests our hearts. You know we never used flattery, nor did we put on a mask to cover up greed—God is our witness. We were not looking for praise from men, not from you or anyone else.[19]

The speaker

I want to finish this chapter, and this book, with two quotes. One is from Lloyd–Jones:

What is speaking? Logic on fire! Eloquent reason![20]

The second is from John Bunyan's *The Pilgrim's Progress*. Bunyan died in 1688. The first edition of his work was published in 1684. The story is about a man, Christian, who journeys from the City of Destruction to the Celestial City. On his way, he comes to the house of the Interpreter who shows him the portrait of the Gospel Preacher:

Christian saw the picture of a very grave person hung up against the wall; and this was the fashion of it. It had eyes lifted up to heaven, the best of books in his hand, the law of truth was written upon his lips, the world was behind his back. It stood as if it pleaded with men, and a crown of gold did hang over his head.[21]

---

19. 1 Thess 2:3–6
20. D Martin Lloyd–Jones, *Preaching and Preachers*, p 97
21. John Bunyan, *The Pilgrim's Progress* (OUP, 1947) p 28

Summary

1. Such is the wonder of the gospel and the desperate need of people that passion and careful explanation go hand in glove in the person who preaches the gospel to others.
2. We show by our words and actions how important we think the gospel is.

—— PART THREE ——

Appendices

The first four appendices that follow contain a selection of talks. They have been included to show how the passage dictates the major thrust of the talk. Other gospel truths are told, but they do not take up as much time as the main point. Please note how this is done.

Each talk is written as I would speak it. This makes it somewhat repetitive and even boring at times, because it is not the way we write. To get the best effect, read the talk aloud. You will get a better 'feel' for it. Better still, see if you can get someone else to read it to you. You will know exactly what it sounds like, and you can spread the blessing in this way!

I have noted the time it takes me to preach them. You will see marks in the margin like this: (5). This means it will take five minutes from the start of the talk to reach this point.

Take note of the introduction. See if it makes you want to listen to the rest of the talk. Notice how the talk moves into the body of the talk and see the transition from point to point. Take note of the way the talk is concluded. Look for the spacing of the illustrations and see if they are apt. See if you can think of ways to improve them.

Appendix V provides some outlines for evangelistic preaching on special occasions, such as Christmas, Easter or weddings. These outlines, of course, will not be appropriate for every such occasion, but they give a flavour of what can be done.

Finally, Appendix VI is a sample self-assessment form for evaluating your own sermons. Use it and adapt it as you see fit.

Forgiveness
and loving God
(LUKE 7:36-50)

I don't know if this has been your experience, but this has been mine. Some people seem to be able to love God without too much difficulty at all and other people seem to find it very hard indeed. Some people seem to be a bit suspicious of God. Some are snaky at him. Others seem to be able to love him without any difficulty at all. I want to try to put my finger on why it is like this.

In 1992, a group of Christian students at Oxford University invited me to give a series of lectures for them on Christianity. Before I spoke each night, one of the undergraduates told us how he or she had become a Christian. On the last night, a young man in a wheel chair was lifted up onto the stage. He manoeuvred himself to a short mic and this was his story as well as I can remember it.

"I have been in this wheelchair since I was eight. It was the result of a family car accident. However that is of no importance. I am reading classics at this university and that also is of no importance. Several years ago my uncle wrote a book called *The Enigma of Suffering*. The book was technical and difficult. By the time I had finished it, I was convinced that God was there and that he was basically good. I asked my uncle if he would recommend further reading. He gave me a book the name of which I have now forgotten. However, as I read it, I discovered that I was a sinful man and in desperate need of forgiveness. I also read that the death of Jesus was sufficient for my total forgiveness. And I availed myself of that forgiveness."

And although it sounded strange he said:

"And I stand before you tonight as a totally forgiven man. **And that is important.** The only other thing I want to say is that God has been so good to me that I want to spend the rest of my life serving him and I think that is important and that is all I have to say."

He wheeled himself to the front of the stage and the ushers lifted him down.

I said to the President of the Christian Union, "That is a very hard act to follow. Do you think I need to say anything more?"

Just sit still for a few minutes and let the full impact of what he said sink in.

If anyone had cause to be angry with God, he did. When he spoke publicly and when I spoke with him privately, it was as if he wasn't disadvantaged at all. How can people rise above things like that and love God? The secret lies in the Bible reading.

(5)   I am going to read Luke 7, from v 36. (Read it)

What I like about the Bible is that it is basically not complicated. It is not like Inspector Morse. The trouble with me is that I am a 'ten on—ten off' TV watcher. Ten minutes awake and ten minutes asleep. When I come up for air with Inspector Morse, there are ten more characters walking around that I haven't seen before. One night

I missed a murder and I couldn't work out what they were on about. However on the other hand if you watch Columbo, you only have to stay awake for the first three minutes. You know who has done the murder, and when I wake up its only a matter as to how far he has bumbled along to the solution. If you don't mind me saying, the Bible stories are more like Columbo than Inspector Morse. It is not very complicated. Only three characters in this story. I want to look at each one because here is the key to loving God.

The first one is Simon the Pharisee. I'm pretty sure that Simon is curious to know if Jesus is a prophet. When the woman breaks down and wets Jesus feet with her tears and wipes them with her hair, he concludes that Jesus cannot be. See verse 39: "If this man were a prophet he would know who was touching him, what kind of woman she is, that she is a sinner." Simon has concluded that Jesus is no different from anyone else. He is not a prophet.

Now the trouble with passing judgement on Jesus is that you pass judgment on yourself at the same time. You're for him—he's for you. You ignore him—he ignores you. You're against him—he's against you. Seems fair, don't you think?

Simon is completely mistaken. Jesus is more than a prophet. He knows exactly what Simon thinks. That's why we have the little parable about the two men who owed money to a moneylender. One owed him $500 and the other $50. Neither could pay, so he forgave them both. Jesus to Simon—"Which one will love him most?"

Simon seems almost grudging with his answer: "I suppose the one who was forgiven most".

"That is exactly right", says Jesus. "You don't think

you need forgiveness? Your heart is like granite. That is why there is so little love. She loves because she has been forgiven much." And Simon is dispensed with. He has been properly ticked off by Jesus.

Ladies and gentlemen, as you listen to me today, if you think that you are all right and that you don't need much forgiveness, then you can be fairly certain that you will get the same treatment from Jesus—because we do need to be forgiven.

The second person we encounter is the woman who, in verse 37, is described as "having lived a sinful life in that town". We don't know exactly what she had done— but it was notorious. Everyone knew about it. Unlike many of my sins, which are hidden, hers were in the open and everyone knew.

(10)   The second thing we know about her was that she had been forgiven by God—and that she had heard about forgiveness from Jesus. That's what the whole story is about. She felt so good that when she heard that Jesus had come to dine with Simon, she worked out a plan to say 'thank you' to Jesus. She'd never properly thanked him and this was her golden opportunity.

I need to interrupt the story to give you some background information. At the time of the Lord Jesus, people did not eat at tables like we do. They had a small table like a coffee table in the middle of the room and from it radiated out couches, like spokes in a wheel. People reclined on the couches with their heads towards the table. They had a cushion under their armpit. They could easily talk to each other across the table and they could reach the food. All the action was at the centre—at the table. If you walked in through the door you would have met a row of bare feet. What the woman decided to do was to nip in and anoint Jesus' feet with the precious ointment and nip out again. By the time the smell of the perfume had filled the room, no-one would know who had done it. Jesus would know. He would have felt it.

However, it didn't quite work out like that. In the heat of the moment her emotions got the better of her and she broke down and began to weep. She let her hair down and started to dry his feet. Suddenly she was in the middle of a theological argy bargy.

I've been in situations where I thought I would be tough, but my emotions have played me false. I feel for this lady. I know what it's like.

But Jesus is full of compassion for her. Although everyone looks down their noses at her, he lifts her up. "Lady, what I told you about forgiveness is true. You really are forgiven. You believed what I said—see in verse 50—your faith has saved you."

That is why she loved much. Because she had been forgiven much.

We don't know where she heard about forgiveness, but we do know that she heard it from Jesus. I can think of a couple of places where this could have happened. Do you remember when Jesus called Levi, the tax collector, to follow him? "You follow me." And he did. Levi threw a party that night and Luke tells us that many tax collectors and sinners came to see and hear Jesus. The Pharisees complained and said, "You can tell a man by the friends he keeps". You can too. They were absolutely right. Thank God he is the friend of sinners. Jesus said, "You don't go to the doctor unless you are sick. I have not come to call the righteous but sinners that they might repent." She might well have been there that night and said to herself, "That's me. I'll do it—I'll repent and get forgiveness."

She might have heard Jesus tell the story of the two men in church. Remember the one up the front—told God how lucky he was to have him on his side. "O God, I thank you that I am not like other men." Do you remember the other man? He stood at the back. He wouldn't lift his face to heaven. He was ashamed in the presence of God. He beat on his chest and cried out, "O God, have pity on me, sinner that I am". Do you remember what Jesus said? "I tell you that **this man—this man**—was in the right with God when he went home." She may well have been there and in her heart she said, "That's me. I'm a sinner." And in her heart she said, "O God, have pity on me".

(Pause).

She knew what it was to be accepted. She felt clean. She was forgiven. It was so good that she risked all with a very expensive gift to say 'thank-you'.

(15)   Ladies and Gentlemen, do you know that experience? Do you know how good it is to be forgiven? Do you know the wonder of being right with God—to be friends with God? If the answer to that is not 'yes' then I am really glad that you are here today. Today is a great day for you to latch onto forgiveness. For the same words of Jesus apply. You can be forgiven. This notorious sinner had known the wonder of forgiveness and she had heard it from Jesus.

I want to stop for a moment and take a step back. I guess that you're not a notorious sinner. Most of us get edgy when there is talk about sin. Many people misunderstand what sin is. When I say that you are a sinful person, I am not making a character judgement on you. I'm not saying that you are a bad person. A sinful person is a person who says 'No' to God, as God. We don't want God to rule over us. We may believe in God and even say prayers, but when push comes to shove, we want to be in charge. Instead of God being in the centre stage of our lives, we move him into the wings. To all intents and purposes, God disappears from our reckoning and we step in and fill the vacuum. We play the role of God. Sometimes we don't even think about this. We just drift into it.

This behaviour is very destructive. You see, if I am pretending to be God and you are pretending to be God, when we meet together who will be God? That puts me on a collision course with you, when really I want to be co-operative. You can see this best with little children. If they can't get their way they just bash each other over the head with the nearest available toy. When we become adults this behaviour is so unsatisfactory. I think the adult way is manipulation. We probably recover quicker from the children's method than the adult one. It is so utterly destructive. This is why God is so cheesed off with us.

I was working in a church in London. One day, one of the men asked me if I would like to have lunch with him. The answer to that is always "Yes".

"At the House of Lords", he added. I thought he might have been a cleaner but he turned out to be a real one. I fronted to the Palace of Westminster on the appointed day. There were two guards in livery.

"You have business in the Palace of Westminster?"

"I am a guest for lunch."

"Your name?"

"John Chapman." Could you believe it? They clicked to attention.

"You are expected, Mr. Chapman. Go through the archway turn to the left and go down the corridor. There is a waiting room there. His Lordship will meet you and I hope you enjoy your lunch."

So I did and he did and I did—in that order. Over lunch, he asked me if I would like to see the Chamber. "We are not sitting at the present moment but I would love to show you around."

It was smaller than I had imagined. The seats face each other and are covered with red leather. In the front is the Wool Sack on which the Lord Chancellor sits. Behind that, six stairs above the ground, is the throne on which the Monarch sits when she comes to address the Lords. It is designed so that, when she is seated, she is head and shoulder above the tallest peers standing. There is no doubt who they think is important here. I said to my friend:

"Would it be all right if I nip up and sit on that chair and you take my photo? It will be a complete smash back in Australia."

The blood drained out of his face.

"It's not on, Chappo."

"It's a joke", I said.

Well I want to tell you it was no joke at all.

Can you imagine that one day you come up for air and discover that there you are as bold as brass and as large as life on God's throne. "Whatever am I doing here? I am not the moral judge of the universe. I didn't create the world. I am not God." What do you think you ought to do? Wouldn't you be wise to get off and lodge an apology and see if it will be accepted? That is what this woman had done when she asked for forgiveness.

(20)   Wouldn't you be wise to do the same and say to God, "I should never have behaved like that. Can you find it in your heart to forgive me?" The wonder of it is he can. Jesus said to this woman, "Your sins are forgiven".

Now what she didn't know then, as you and I do now, is that by the time we get to the end of this Gospel,

Jesus is on the cross, bearing our sins, taking the punishment that my sins deserved.

As I come to the end of this talk, I wonder if you would picture in your mind Jesus on the cross. You will have seen pictures of this. There is Jesus in the centre with a thief on either side. He is crying out, "My God! My God! Why have you forsaken me?"

What's going on? Isn't he the Son of God? How can he be God-forsaken?

The Bible tells us that Jesus, who was without sin, took the punishment that our sins deserve so that we can be totally forgiven—become friends with God.

Isn't that something?

No wonder she came back to say thanks. She was overwhelmed by the wonder of forgiveness—how much more us who know what it cost!

As you have been listening to me, you may have said in your heart, "I am like that woman. I need forgiveness."

I'll ask God for that now.

I am going to pray a prayer. It is designed for people who want to do just that. It won't be applicable for everyone—so let me tell you what I am going to say and you can work out if it is a good prayer for you.

I will say:

Heavenly Father, I haven't served you as God. I am sorry about this. From today onwards I want to change. Please help me to live that way. Lord Jesus, thank you for dying on the cross so that I can be forgiven. Please forgive me for everything. Please take over the running of my life.

Let me tell you how I will pray this prayer. I will pray it sentence by sentence, then pause. If it is yours, why not echo it to God in your head. If this isn't your prayer, why not say something to God that is appropriate to your situation.

Let us pray.

> Heavenly Father,
> I haven't served you as God.
> I am sorry about this.
> From today onwards I want to change.
> Please help me to live that way.
> Lord Jesus, thank you for dying on the cross
> so that I can be forgiven
> Please forgive me for everything.
> Please take over the running of my life.
> Amen.

Life was not meant to be empty

(JOHN 4:3-26)

I enjoy life and the older I get the more I seem to enjoy it. I have had a full and exciting life. I have been spared great tragedy. And I have been spared much drudgery.

Now I'm not so foolish as to know that this is not the lot of all people. So what qualifies me to speak on the subject of *Life was not meant to be empty*? Only by sticking to the Bible—that's what qualifies me. Here God tells all of us what life is about.

Christianity is all about Jesus, and he said, "I have come that you might have life—life in all its fullness".

Do you know that the first miracle that Jesus performed was a 'fun' miracle? At a wedding in a small country town when they ran out of wine, Jesus turned water into wine—and more than they could use!

Before I became a Christian, I thought that Christianity was a dreary no-good affair. I was totally mistaken.

In the Bible passage I am about to read, we meet a women whose life is **Empty**. And she is also **Hurting**. She meets Jesus and she learns, first hand, that life is not meant to be empty.

Let me read the first part of this story to you from the Bible. I am reading from John, Chapter 4, at the sentence with the number '7'. Jesus and his disciples are travelling from Jerusalem through the countryside of Samaria. They arrive at a well, which is outside the village of Sychar. Jesus rests there while the disciples go into the village to get food to eat. I pick up the story at number 7:

(Read John 4:7–15)

It is a strange conversation. They don't seem to be on the same wavelength, do they? Jesus is talking about the gift of God and running water and eternal life. She seems to be talking about the water in the well and the emptiness and the drudgery of living.

I remember once, when I was living in Armidale in NSW, I visited a friend who was in hospital in Sydney. He was very deaf. It is hard to carry on a private conversation in a hospital ward with a deaf person:

Mr Gee, at the top of his lungs:

"How good to see you John. How did you come down?"

"By car, Mr. Gee."

"O! By train", he bellowed back.

I raised my voice and shouted, "I came down by car".

"I like coming in that air-conditioned train. It is so comfortable."

I gave up. The man in the bed next to Mr Gee was laughing so much I thought he would have a relapse. I always think about this when I read the story of this woman and Jesus. They aren't really on the same wavelength.

(5) As she approaches the well, Jesus asks her for a drink. This would have been unheard of. Men did not speak

publicly to a woman—specially a stranger—and Jews did not speak to Samaritans under any circumstances. That is why she is so shaken. "How come you, a Jewish man, ask for a drink from me, a Samaritan?"

"O Lady! If you really knew who you were talking to, and if you knew the gift of God, you would ask me to give you the living—the running water." What is he talking about? There was no stream there. He is on about something else. And what is the gift of God? At this stage, we don't know any more than she does.

The woman:

"Go on! Who do you think you are? If you could give the living water you wouldn't be asking me for a drink. Who **do** you think you are?"

Jesus:

"Everyone who drinks of this water will be thirsty again. But whoever drinks of the water that I give will never thirst. Indeed, it will become in him a spring of water welling up into eternal life."

It sounds fantastic. But what does it mean? Never thirst? Eternal life? It's obviously not physical.

Do you think he is talking about (pause) fulfilment in life? Never thirsting! Isn't he saying something like, "I can give you satisfaction in life"? He's talking about being fulfilled as a person (pause) living life as we were meant to, isn't he? And he said that he gives it to people. It is the gift of God. And it ends up in eternal life. It's big— perhaps too big for her to understand. Eternal life! Not only life that goes on for ever—but life that has a God-quality about it. Life that is lived in relationship with God. It's big! It's mind-bending!

Do you think that you have this—this God quality? Do you know what it is to be friends with God?

She misses the point entirely. She says, "My life is empty and full of disappointment and drudgery! Please give me this water so that I won't have to come day after day after day to this well."

Jesus hardly ever gives us what we ask for when there is something better for us that we just didn't know about. Love always acts like that. He takes her at her word. He wants to give her the gift of God. He wants to give her eternal life!

Now what follows is a real shock. So totally unexpected. Let me read it to you.

(Read John 4:16–26)

What a poor creature she is? Her life is empty. Her longing for love and relationship and security have all come to nothing. And she is hurting.

(10)   "Go home and call your husband." He wants her to face the truth—admit she was wrong—and start again.

"I have no husband." It is too painful! It hurts too much!

But he knows. He really does care. That's the way he is.

Oh, by the way, it is exactly like that with us. We cannot have eternal life while we try to run our lives our way. We need to run them his way. I wonder if you had been in the shoes of this woman what Jesus would have said to you? What, for you, gets in the way of Jesus being first in your life? Family? A special relationship, that you know is wrong and does not please God? Work? Or maybe money? Is it being popular? Or just the independent spirit, that won't let Jesus be first in your life? Whatever it is—don't run for cover. There isn't anywhere to hide. You may say, "I have no husband", but he will say, "I know. I know exactly what you are like. Don't fight me. Let me give you the gift of God. Let me give you eternal life. I won't if you put other things before me."

For her, it was the endless searching for happiness and life-satisfaction in relationships. How she wanted to be loved. Can you imagine the hurting? "You have had five husbands and the man you are living with now is not your husband." She hadn't even gone through the motions this time. She would live with anyone.

We don't know if the five had died or divorced her. Whichever way it was, it must have hurt terribly. It might have been for this very reason that Jesus sought her out. It was love that put its finger on the sorest spot of all. It is very personal. But that's the way he is. He doesn't pretend and he doesn't want us to pretend.

Now what happens is fascinating. She runs for cover and she does it in two of the most common ways I know. First she tries religious controversy and then, procrastination.

Did you notice the moment Jesus put his finger on her sin, she said, "Well, I'd believe if there weren't so many denominations." No that's not right—but she might just as well have. What she did start to talk about was a raging religious controversy of their day. She just wanted to get off the hook.

I know lots of people who are like that. They use excuses that they think are good reasons for not having Jesus first in their lives. But Jesus knows. If you are like this, give yourself a break. Admit it! While there is still time.

Her second method of escape is: leave it till later.

"I know when Messiah comes, he will tell us everything."

She's saying something like, "There is no hurry. We can deal with this later."

Jesus says, "NO! Don't delay. I who speak to you am he."

I am happy to tell you that she did come good and you can read that for yourself in John, Chapter 4 from number 27 onwards.

But as I close, let me say to you that if you have been delaying in coming to Jesus then there is no future in that. There is no good reason. Jesus has shown that he is the Son of God. He really is God's king, Messiah. He died on the cross so that we can be forgiven. His death was to deal with the fact that we have allowed other things to displace Jesus' rightful place as first for us. He took the punishment that we deserved and he says, "Today if you hear my voice, do not harden your heart". We know that Jesus rose again from the dead. He is now at God's right hand and he will judge us at the end on the judgement day.

(15)   That is why he says do **not** delay. Take action **now**. Today!

It is possible that, as you have been listening to me, you in many ways have been able to identify with this woman. Perhaps you've said, "My life is empty and I now know why".

Perhaps you are hurting and you have discovered that there's the possibility of healing and a fresh start.

Why don't you do the right thing and turn back to Jesus and seek his forgiveness and ask him for the gift of eternal life.

I am going to pray a prayer. Listen while I tell you what is in it and see if it would be an appropriate one for you.

I will say:

Dear Lord Jesus I have not had you as first in my life. I am truly sorry about this. Thank you for dying for me so that I can be forgiven. Please forgive me. Please give me the gift of eternal life. Please take over the running of my life.

Is that your prayer? Let me tell you how I will pray it.

I will say each sentence and stop. I will leave time for you to echo it to God inside your head. If this prayer is not appropriate for you, why not say something to God now that is right for you?

Let us pray.

Dear Lord Jesus,
I have not had you as first in my life.
I am truly sorry about this.
Thank you for dying for me so that I can be
    forgiven.
Please forgive me.
Please give me the gift of eternal life.
Please take over the running of my life.
Amen.

(18)

Nothing recedes like success

(Luke 12:16-21)

I wonder if you would consider that your life was successful.

I'm not asking if you have been successful in the past or if you think that you might get your act together some time in the future? But are you successful now? Today?

Some people have been told so often that they are successful that it never crosses their mind to doubt it.

Some have been so regularly put-down that they would never dream of saying, "Yes."

Success is a really hard thing to define isn't it? What would you judge success by? Money? Work? Marriage? Family? Or all of these put together?

It's hard isn't it?

I am going to read you a story that Jesus told in the Bible about a man who I think everyone would have thought was very successful. God, on the other hand, had other ideas.

O! And by the way, I think he was probably an Australian. Listen and see what you think. It comes from Luke's gospel at Chapter 12 and I am reading from the sentence numbered "16".

(Read Luke 12:16–21)

Well, what do you think? Is he Australian? Listen again.

What a lucky man you are. Take life easy, eat, drink, and be merry.

He's got to be one, doesn't he? O well. Maybe not!

He is an interesting man and the story is a cautionary one. It says: Take care! Life isn't always the way it seems.

I think the man made two fundamental mistakes.

The first mistake was: **He lived as if God wasn't there.**

The Bible says, "The fool has said in his heart, 'There is no God'". And God's judgement on the man was just that. **What a fool you are.**

We hardly know anything about this man. We don't know if he was good or whether he was bad. We don't know if he was industrious or whether he was bone-lazy. We don't know if he was a faithful husband or a woman-iser. We don't know if he was a good father or a child-beater. All we know is that he was not rich towards God. That's what tipped the balance.

If you had met this man in the street and asked him if he believed in God, he might easily have said 'Yes'. But in the day-to-day living, he went on as if God was not there. He is at the centre of his life. He consults himself about the decisions of life. He is in charge. Listen to him:

> I will tear down the barn and build bigger ones, where I will store the grain and all my other goods. Then I will say to myself: **Lucky man!** **You** have all the good things **you** need for many years. Take life easy, eat, drink, and be merry.

It is a common mistake to live as if God isn't there and it is foolish as well because **God really is there.** He has shown himself.

I used to teach RI at a Sydney High school. You could be absolutely certain that with each new class I had, someone—sooner or later—would say, "Hey! Have you ever seen God?"

It's a clever question because he thinks that I will have to say 'No'. My answer was, "I could have if I'd been on time". You can't live in every moment of history, can you? I never saw Queen Victoria although most of them thought that I qualified!

(5)   But had I been there in first century Palestine I could have seen and heard Jesus. I could have seen God.

What a very impressive man he was! Do you remember the time when he was teaching from the back of Peter's boat and afterward they crossed the Sea of Galilee?

A furious storm came up. Jesus was asleep. The disciples were in despair for their lives. One of them shook him and woke him. "Don't you care if we all perish?" He stood up in the back of the boat and said to the wind "STOP" and to the waves "DOWN! DOWN." Mark, in his Gospel, tells us that there was a great calm and the disciples were goggle-eyed and said, "Who is this man that the winds and the waves obey him?". It's fairly impressive, don't you think? Any day you think that you are the master of the creation, take a trip to Manly in the ferry. When you come to that part where the ferry crosses the heads and the swell is at its greatest, why not give it a go yourself? I'd do it quietly from the back, if I were you, you won't be so embarrassed. Nothing's going to happen.

Do you remember the time the little girl, Jairus' daughter, has just died and Jesus takes her by the hand and says, "Little girl. I say to you arise" and she did? That's pretty impressive. The son of the widow of Nain was in his coffin. They had finished the service and were taking him out to bury him. Jesus stopped the procession and said, "Young man I say to you—Arise!" and the dead man sat up in his coffin. Now that is impressive! I've taken hundreds of funerals in my time. It has never occurred to me to rap on the casket and say, "Young man, I say to you—Arise!" because I know that nothing well happen—apart from the fact that I will add more trauma to those who are mourning. I'm not the Lord of life and death. I can't call the dead to life. I'm not God.

A centurion had a slave who was sick. He sent a message to Jesus and asked him to come and heal him. Jesus agreed and set off for the house. Before he got there, the centurion sent a messenger to Jesus, "I am not worthy for you to come under my roof. But I am a man in authority. I know what it is to give orders and to be obeyed. And I recognise that you are a man in authority. Just speak a word and my servant will be well." So Jesus did, and he was. Isn't that incredible? He wasn't even near the man. He did it by the movement of his mind. It is so impressive!

The trouble with me is that I heard all these stories when I was a child in Sunday School and in my mind they were all muddled up with Winnie-the-Pooh and the great-grey-green-greasy Limpopo river all dotted around with fever trees. It wasn't until I became a man that I realised how very impressive each of these incidents were. To say nothing of how impressive they are collectively.

Jesus says that the reason he is able to do these things is because he is God, God-in-the-flesh. We know that God is there because of Jesus. He isn't hiding. He has stepped out of the shadows into the blazing sunlight of the person of Jesus. No wonder God said to this man, "**What a fool you are**".

Not only did God show himself to us in Jesus but he

showed us exactly the sort of person he is and how much he loves us. He allowed Jesus to die in our place and take the punishment that our sins deserve. For years and years, I didn't know that. I knew that Jesus had died on the cross. But I didn't know that it had anything to do with me! I didn't know that it was so that I could be forgiven and become friends with God. I didn't know that God loved me like that. I thought that if you lived a good life everything would be OK. I was completely mistaken. I, like the man in the story, was a fool. I was careless about God and I needed to be forgiven. And Jesus loved me and gave his life for me. Thank God he is a kind and loving God.

(10) When I was a child, I went to Sunday school. Each year we went on a picnic to the Royal National Park. There were rowing boats that could be hired. There was much fun to be had in hurling water over each other and generally mucking around. One year a small boy who couldn't swim fell out of a boat into the water. A teacher who couldn't swim jumped into the water to save him. I can't imagine that. I could swim when I was 6. This man just jumped in. He grabbed the lad and 'threw' him towards the boat. The kids in the boat put out an oar and he grabbed it and pulled himself in. Meanwhile the teacher's legs had got caught in the weeds and the current had moved him under water. The boat drifted away from the spot and by the time the kids had called for help, 3/4 hour had elapsed before they recovered the body. We never went there again. It was a terrible tragedy.

That little boy was slightly younger than me so I guess now he would be about 65. I don't know if he ever thinks about it, but if this morning when he woke up he said to himself, "I am alive today because Mr. Brooks died for me" you wouldn't think he was exaggerating would you?

Jesus death was just like that. I can say today, "I am forgiven and alive towards God because Jesus died for me".

No wonder God says to this man, **"What a fool you are!"**

This man was rich—very rich indeed—in everything—except the only thing that really mattered. **He was not rich towards God.**

It is a cautionary tale. It's designed for us to sit up and take notice.

Don't make the mistake that he made. If you have been living as if God isn't there then be thankful because there is still time for you to stop and turn around. Start serving God as your God. Let him have first place in your life. Thank him for sending Jesus to die for you. Put your trust in the Lord Jesus and let him forgive you before it is too late.

Which brings me to the second fatal mistake he made. **He lived as if there was no judgement day.**

He doesn't seem to have given much thought to his death! He has made provision for his life but not for life after death. Although he has 'much goods laid up for many years'—he doesn't have any years left to enjoy them. In fact, he doesn't have any time at all.

He is a fool!

And Jesus warns us, "So it is with everyone who is not rich towards God."

This man plunged into eternity totally unprepared.

Several years ago, I read this short article in the *Sydney Morning Herald*. It was on page 57! Its headline was **Schoolboy killed in explosion.**

Let me read it to you.

A 16-year old school boy on a work experience

program was killed yesterday in an explosion at
Muswellbrook, in the Hunter Valley. Police said
Peter Simon Richards of Muswellbrook, was
struck on the head by a piece of metal after a small
explosion in a refrigerator repair shop.

That's all it is! A few lines in the back of the *Sydney
Morning Herald*.

What a tragedy! 16 years old! Do you think he would
have given any thought to eternity that morning before he
left for work? I doubt it! It was probably the last thing on
his mind. But before the day was out he was in the presence of his Maker.

(15)   It is so hard for us to come to terms with the fact that
we are not immortal. That we, too, will die.

Had I been in Peter Simon Richard's shoes and
plunged into eternity, I would have heard those terrifying
words "You fool!". At age 16, I was totally careless about
the things of God. I was totally unprepared for death, let
alone life after death. How thankful I am that I lived long
enough to repent and become rich towards God.

There are two indisputable facts of life:

1.   All of us here will one day die. Of that there is no
       doubt!

2.   None of us knows when that will happen!

Given this information, what do you think the wise
person should do? Be ready all the time?

This man's mistakes were very serious. They cost him
a place in eternity.

It's meant as a warning. Did you hear what Jesus said?
"So it is with everyone who is not rich towards God."

Could that just be you? As you have been listening,
you've said to yourself, "That's me. I'm not really rich

towards God." If that's you then today is a good day to rectify that.

I am going to pray a prayer for people like that to become wise in God's eyes. Let me tell you what I am going to say and you will be able to judge if this is a good prayer for you.

I will say:

Dear Heavenly Father, I have been living as if you were not there.

I have not had you at the centre of my life. Please help me to change. Dear Lord Jesus, thank you for dying for me. Please forgive me. Please take over the running of my life and make me rich towards you.

Let me tell you how I will pray this prayer. I will say each sentence and then pause. If it is yours, why not echo it to God inside your head and it will be truly yours. If this prayer isn't yours, then why not say something to God that is appropriate to your situation.

Let us pray:

> Dear Heavenly Father,
> I have been living as if you were not there.
> I have not had you at the centre of my life.
> Please help me to change.
> Dear Lord Jesus, thank you for dying for me.
> Please forgive me.
> Please take over the running of my life and make me rich towards you.
> Amen.

Responding positively to God

(1 THESSALONIANS 1:9-10)

Some facts that come to us don't require any action at all. If I say to you "Canberra is the capital of Australia" you don't have to do anything. It isn't life changing!

However, if I say, "There is a time-bomb under this building and it is due to go off in 5 minutes" that is a different matter altogether. You will have to take action now. I guess you have two options. You can leave quickly or you can sit tight and hope for the best! Whichever you choose, posterity will judge your wisdom or otherwise.

When it comes to Christians, there are two facts that are presented to us and they are of the time-bomb variety rather than in the Canberra is the capital of Oz category.

These two facts are:

1. **God has shown himself**—that he is there.
2. **Jesus died, rose again, and is alive now.**

Let me say them again:

1. **God has shown himself**—that he is there.
2. **Jesus died, rose again, and is alive now.**

I heard a man tell a story about a birthday party he

had been invited to. He told us that he had been brought up in the Western Suburbs of Sydney. He said, "When I went to Sydney University a whole new world opened up to me. I discovered that people lived quite differently to me. One day I received an invitation to a Birthday Party. That in itself was a novelty. Where I came from, you learned about parties by word of mouth and just fronted up. No-one invited you. Certainly not with a formal invitation. On the bottom left-hand corner of the invitation it had these words: 'Dress—Black Tie'. I was glad because I only owned one tie and it was black. I got it out that morning and my Mum ironed it. When I got to the party I realised that 'Black Tie' did **NOT** mean black tie. It meant a dinner jacket and a black bow tie or a tuxedo." He said, "It was the longest night I could remember".

Do you think it is possible to know exactly how God wants us to react to the two facts that he is there and that Jesus has died and risen again?

Thankfully he has told us exactly how to do this. Isn't that a relief?

There is a perfect illustration for us in the Bible. A group of people who live in Thessalonica are held up to us as a model in their response. Let me read it to you.

(Read 1 Thessalonians 1:9–10)

Did you notice that they did two things? They reacted to the fact that God had shown himself by:

Turning to God from idols to serve the true and living God.

The Apostle Paul had visited them and had explained to them about Jesus.

We don't know exactly what he said. But there is no doubt that he would have told them that Jesus was the Son of God—that God had chosen to show to the world exactly what he was like in this man. He would have explained that Jesus was master in God's world and that he demonstrated this in the way he healed the sick, raised the dead, cut through religious humbug and got straight to the heart of the matter. He claimed to be able to forgive sins and also that he would judge all people at the end of the age. These were enormous claims but he was able to back them up. Whenever he saw people in need, irrespective of its nature, he was able to put the broken pieces together again. His actions were described as "he went around doing good and healing all those who were oppressed by the devil".

What a novelty this message must have been.

Prior to this, the people of Thessalonica had been idol worshippers. They had worshipped the Greco-Roman gods who they thought lived on Mt Olympus.

I guess their worship would have been a bit like ours. Some would have been devout. Some would have been sceptical—uncertain. Others were careless. And some went along with it to keep their wives happy. And still others were bewildered not knowing quite what to believe.

(5) But whatever they thought before—after they had heard the apostle Paul, they said, "I have been mistaken". Some might have said, "I have been wilful". Others, "I have been careless". And I guess some said, "At last! Now I know which way to go."

Whatever they had been, they responded by turning their back on their idols. They said, "NO. This is not the way." They turned to God—God as he was revealed in the Lord Jesus. They turned from their idols and decided to serve the true and living God. The God who is alive. He has acted in the past, but he is still there—the living God—who acts now in the present.

And this is the way God wants people to react to him.

I guess for us idolatry is not a big thing. I'd be surprised if you have an idol or a family shrine—although I know that that is not impossible.

Idolatry in the Western world at the end of the 20th century usually takes a more sophisticated form.

If I were to ask you:

"What are you living for?"

"What is the most important thing in life for you?"

"What do you want for your children that you could not get for yourself?"

If the answers to these questions don't focus into the person and work of Jesus, then I think you have an idol. Your God is not the true and living God.

It could be status—a desire to be well thought of— prestige. It could as simple as wanting to get on with people, so that you go along with any idea at all. It could be the family—work—making money—the kids. Or all of these put together.

Whatever it is, we too need to recognise that life is about serving the true and living God—who has shown himself in Jesus.

For me, I had to come to terms with the fact that I was not God and turn my back on idolatry and say 'Yes' to God-in-Christ.

Have you done that? How have you responded to the fact that God is there? He is alive and well. He expects us to respond to him in an appropriate manner. You may have to say, "I've been mistaken" or "I've been careless" or maybe "I've been wilful". Whatever it is, today is a good day to do it.

The second fact that the Thessalonians responded to was that Jesus had died, was buried and came back to life again—and is now alive.

This is how they reacted:

They waited for his Son from heaven, whom he raised from the dead—Jesus, who rescues us from the coming wrath.

There is no doubt that Paul told the Thessalonians about the death of Jesus. He would have explained to them that his death was not an ordinary one. It was special. It was to bear away the sin of the world.

This is how Jesus, himself, described it: "This is my blood which is shed for the forgiveness of sins".

On another occasion he said, "I am the good shepherd. The good shepherd lays down his life for the sheep." Again he said, "The reason why my father loves me is because I lay down my life for the sheep". And on yet another occasion, "I have come to give my life as a ransom for many".

One of the apostles describes it as: "He himself bore our sins in his body on the tree"—on the cross.

The reason for this is really simple to grasp. We have said 'No' to God as God over us. This behaviour is very destructive.

(10)   When I won't have God ruling my life, I cannot relate to you properly. I don't even treat myself properly and I don't relate to the rest of the world properly. I set myself up as God. The Bible says that this attitude is the source of all our problems.

It mightn't matter so much if it wasn't for the fact that God is passionately concerned with how I treat you. He is concerned with how I treat me. And he has never lost interest in the whole world. What we do with it matters to him.

The Bible says that we will answer for the way be have lived. It tells us that God is rightly angry when we hurt people and our world. It hurts him. His wrath will come on us.

However this is not the end. Jesus took the punishment, that our sins deserve, when he died on the cross. Do you remember that terrible cry from the cross, "My God! My God! Why have you forsaken me?" Here, Jesus was bearing away the sin of the world. Yours—mine—Old Uncle Tom Cobbly's and All. This is staggering news!

One year my Aunty Millie gave me a magnifying class for Christmas. Her knowledge of juvenile delinquency was very poor indeed. She thought that I would have loads of fun making little things bigger! I did have quite a bit of fun doing that. But when I got it into the sunlight— that was another matter altogether.

You could set alight to a small leaf. You could set alight a bigger leaf. The *Sydney Morning Herald*!

I burned my name into the front gate—which gave my father no joy at all.

However, when I burned down the chicken house, my father said, "Enough is enough". I never saw that magnifying glass again.

They are amazing aren't they? You can come out into the open on a sunny morning and the warmth of the sun makes you feel great. You can take a magnifying glass and 'bend' the rays of the sun into such a sharp point of intensity that the power generated burns things.

Try to imagine an enormous moral magnifying glass through which was passed all punishment due for all the sins of the world. Yours—mine—6,000,000 through the gas chambers—the killing fields of Cambodia—rape, pillage, carnage!

Imagine that we can drag it down—down—down until it reaches one person—in one moment of time—with such terrible intensity.

Listen to the agonised cry. "My God! My God! Why? Why–have–you–forsaken me?"

When you see this, you soon realise that there is no other way to be forgiven or God would not have chosen that one.

The Thessalonians responded by trusting that God would forgive them because of the death of Jesus. They believed that Jesus rescued them from **God's wrath to come**.

Not only had they been told that Jesus died for them, but they were also told that Jesus had conquered death. He came back to life and was now in heaven and was coming back to bring about the judgement of God.

The death of Jesus had really worked.

He was now king.

He would return as judge.

They waited with confidence. Whenever Jesus chose to return, they were ready.

If it was today—they were ready.

If it was in ten years—they were ready.

If they died and met Jesus in judgement—**they were ready**.

(15)   This talk has almost finished. As I close, can I ask you how you have responded to the death and resurrection of the Lord Jesus?

Have you ever said, "I can't make myself good enough for God. I will put my trust in the fact that Jesus died and rose again for my forgiveness."

Tonight would be a good night to do that. To respond like the Thessalonians did. To turn to God and serve him. To trust Jesus for complete forgiveness.

I am going to pray a prayer. It is a prayer for people who say, "I haven't responded positively to the fact that

God has shown himself in Jesus. But today I will turn from the idols and serve the living and true God and I will put my trust in Jesus the deliverer." This prayer won't be appropriate for everyone, but it could just be just right for you. Listen and see if it is.

I will say:

Dear Heavenly Father, I haven't been serving you. From today onwards, I want to serve you, the true and living God. Please help me to do that. Lord Jesus, thank you for dying and rising for me. Please forgive me. Thank you for taking my punishment. Please help me to keep trusting you.

This is how I will pray this prayer. I will say it sentence by sentence and stop. If it is your prayer why not echo it to God inside your own head. If for some reason it is not for you why not say something to God which is appropriate for your situation.

Let us pray.

> Dear Heavenly Father,
> I haven't been serving you.
> From today onwards, I want to serve you, the
>   true and living God.
> Please help me to do that.
> Lord Jesus, thank you for dying and rising for me.
> Please forgive me.
> Thank you for taking my punishment.
> Please help me to keep trusting you.
> Amen.

Some outlines for special occasions

At Christmas
Bible Passage: Luke 2:1–11

Introduction
One of our problems at Christmas is that everyone knows the story—Mary—Joseph—Three Wise Men—Donkeys —and the baby in the manger.

- How come such a simple story could have hung around for 2,000 years?
- God tells us why the event is so important. He (through the angel) tells us what it all means.
- Why not check out your understanding against his?

Read the Bible: Luke 2:1–11

Body
Did you notice that God tells us two important features about Christmas?

State the point **Christmas is about being rescued**

Read the Bible: v 11

Explain it
- This very night your rescuer has been born – your saviour has been born.
- A rescuer implies that we need to be rescued.
- All of us have turned our back on God. We have not acknowledged that God has rights over us. We might believe in God—we just don't want him to be God over us.
- We need to be rescued from the results of this behaviour etc.
- The baby in the manger was that rescuer. He grew to be a man. He showed he was the Son of God. He took the punishment that our sins deserved etc.

Illustrate it

Apply it
- It is good news of great joy for all people.

State the point **Christmas is about Jesus being King**

Read the Bible: v 11 'A Saviour who is Christ the Lord.'

Explain it
- Christ is not a surname—it is a job description—like Bill the Plumber
- Christ means anointed one. Who gets anointed? Priest and Kings.
- This little baby in the manger is the King over God's world.
- He is that now.

Illustrate it

Apply it
- Someone *is* in charge. We will all meet him as judge at the end and give an account of our lives. That's why it is so important to know him as Saviour.
- Christmas can be bad news of no joy to people who continue to rebel against this King.

Conclusion

Why not make this Christmas the best Christmas yet?
Latch onto forgiveness through Jesus – and
Bow the knee to Jesus as *your* king.

At Easter
Bible Passage: Luke 24:36–48

Introduction

Can you imagine the shock! You are with friends at dinner. A mutual friend has just died. You are talking about him. Suddenly he appears with you in the room as large as life. Well! Larger than life! What a shock!

Let me read the story to you.

Read the Bible: Luke 24:36–48

Body

Let me fill in some of the background to this story.

Background Facts

1. Jesus was crucified and was buried in the garden tomb.
2. The tomb was empty.
3. An angel told the women at the empty tomb that Jesus was alive. He had risen from the dead.
4. Two of the disciples had met Jesus as they were on their way home to the village of Emmaus.

5. Now Jesus is there in their midst—not a ghost—
   he is there larger than life.
   - But what does it mean? Jesus tells us the
     meaning.
   - There are three imperatives.

State the point **Everything about Jesus in the scriptures
must be fulfilled**

Read the Bible: v 44

Explain it
The entire Bible is about Jesus and all of it must be
fulfilled. From God's point of view it is unthinkable that
it would not be so etc.

llustrate it

Apply it

State the point **Jesus must suffer and rise from the dead**

Read the Bible: v 46

Explain it
   - Everything about Jesus focuses into his death and
     resurrection.
   - They are at the centre of all God's activities etc.
   - Why is this so etc?

llustrate it

Apply it

State the point **Repentance and forgiveness of sins must
be preached**

Read the Bible: v 47

Explain it
It must happen. It is not an optional extra. It must happen to us and for us etc.

llustrate it

Apply it

Conclusion
Is repentance and faith a reality for you etc?

On Anzac Day (or Remembrance Day)
Bible Passage: Romans 5:7-8

Introduction
Today is a day when we specially think about those who fought and died on our behalf so that freedom can be a reality for us.
- (Some story of heroism could be told here)
- Freedom was their best hope for us. For that they were prepared to make a great sacrifice. Some with their life.
- Do you think that such a thing is easy?
- Let me read the Bible to you and see how such a sacrifice is viewed.

Read the Bible: Romans 5:7-8

Body
See what it says?

State the point **It is a difficult thing to die for a friend**

Read the Bible: v 7

Explain it
- As difficult as it is, it can be done.

- And it has been done etc.

llustrate it

Apply it

State the point **God does it for his enemies**

Read the Bible: v 8

Explain it
- It is mind blowing!
- Christ died for us—He did it when we were his enemies etc!

llustrate it

Apply it

Conclusion
We have all benefited from the death of soldiers who have died and today is a day to honour their memory.

Have you benefited from the death of the Lord Jesus' sacrifice etc?

At A Wedding
Bible Reading: Ephesians 5:25-29

Introduction
(Talk of the happiness of this day)
- This man and this woman are today formalizing the special relationship into which they are entering.
- Relationships are easier to experience than they are to define. What is relationship? What is a good one? What is a bad one? How can you tell the difference?

- All genuine and true relationships take their pattern from the way in which God relates to us in Christ. How is that?

Read the Bible: Ephesians 5:25

Body

State the point **God relates to us by serving us**

Explain it
- He does this in the death of Jesus.
- Jesus dies so that we can come back and start relating to God properly.
- (Explain how this works etc.)
- How does God relate to us? He loves us and serves us. He has our best interest at heart. He does it to his own disadvantage. So husbands are to love and serve their wives even to their own disadvantage.

Illustrate it

Apply it
- How do we relate to God? We accept his service with love and thankfulness. So wives relate to their husbands.

Conclusion
It is hard to follow God's blueprint for relationship if we haven't experienced relationship with God. There is all the world of difference between knowing someone and knowing about someone.

At a Funeral

(I would speak briefly, or get someone else to speak, about the deceased at a different slot in the service before the talk. This enables us to concentrate on the teaching of the Bible.)

Bible Passage: Luke 23:39-43

Introduction
Death comes to all of us
- This day reminds us, more than anything, of our own mortality. It is a good day on which to give serious thought to our own death and to ensure that we are prepared for it—that it doesn't take us by surprise.
- Let me read from the Bible some very reassuring words that Jesus spoke to a man who was facing death.
- He was not a good man. In fact, he was the opposite. He had lived a bad life and was now facing his death and soon his Maker.

Read the Bible: Luke 23:39–43

Let me give some background to this incident.
- This is the day that Jesus died. He had been nailed to his cross as had two thieves and murderers. One on either side of him. Those around the cross —on the ground—were mocking Jesus etc.
- All three men were facing death. They knew and had time to prepare.
- The reactions of these two men to Jesus at the point of their death are very different. They show us the difference between the wise and the foolish person.

Body

State the point **One man treats Jesus as his servant**
Read the Bible: v 39

Explain it

- See what he is saying? Save yourself and save me. He treats God like his servant. We have all acted like this. We move God from the rightful place at the centre of our lives. We believe he is there but don't react to him as God. Sometimes, in difficulty, we pray. We treat him like a servant.
- This man is indifferent to the fact that he is about to meet Jesus in judgement. He is unready and so close. It is tragic.

Illustrate it

Apply it

State the point **One Man treats Jesus as a King**

Read the Bible: v 42

Explain it

- Instead of treating Jesus as *his servant*, he sees himself *to be a servant* of Jesus. "Remember me when you come as King."
- Jesus never looked less like a king than he did at this moment. Yet he is exercising his power against his greatest enemy (and ours). Jesus is taking the punishment that our sins deserve. He is setting us free from sin and death and the power of Satan etc.
- The man is given the best promise any person can hear and particularly when they face death.

Illustrate it

Apply it

State the point "Today after you and I are dead, we will be together in paradise."

Read the Bible: v 43

Explain it
He is given a promise of eternal life.
He doesn't know how this can happen, but we do.
He didn't know that Jesus' death on the cross was for him. But we do etc.

Illustrate it

Apply it

Conclusion
At death, everything depends on how we have reacted to Jesus.

Today is a very good day to say to Jesus, "Please remember me now that you are King."

Today is a great day to reflect on this and to be ready for that day, whenever it comes.

At a Celebration
Bible Reading: 1 Timothy 6:17-19

Introduction
- Do you think God is a happy person or a glum person?
- Does he enjoy himself or is he against everything we enjoy?
- I used to think of God as being against enjoyment. It is strange, but I used to think of him as a sort of a

226

policeman. [You won't be able to use this if it isn't true for you. You will have to use an alternative like, "I have met people who think of God like etc."]

- Strange, isn't it, because that is completely wrong.
- Let me read something from the Bible that shows how different God is.

Read the Bible: 1 Timothy 6:17

Body

State the point **God has made everything for our enjoyment!** *Can you believe it?*

Explain it

- The world around us. (Tell them about your favourite sight. Niagara in the spring. Seven-mile beach on a sunny morning. Sunset on the western plains of NSW.) And God did it for our enjoyment.
- God not only provided us with things to enjoy, but people. People who do clever things and can produce beautiful things that give us so much fun and joy. People who love us and who we can love.
- Do you know that song of Louis Armstrong – *What a wonderful world*?
- I feel like singing it.
- Wait on! Didn't they sing that in the background to *Good Morning Vietnam*? They did. Suddenly I am brought back to earth. I mustn't start romanticising. The real world is all muddled up with the good and the bad.

Illustrate it

Apply it

State the point **Why is that so?**

(Introduce sin and how it spoils the world God made for our enjoyment etc.)

Explain it
- You might have thought that God would have given us up.
- We probably would have if we had been in God's place, but thankfully he isn't like us.
- He sent his Son into the world to die etc. He wants to forgive us, to draw us into friendship with him and to enjoy him and his world properly.

Illustrate it

Apply it

Conclusion
Would you describe your relationship with God as an enjoyable one? Do you think God enjoys it? It might be worth changing?

Assessment form

*Here is a self-assessment form
you can use when you listen to a tape
of your talk.*

PREACHER SELF-ASSESSMENT SHEET

PASSAGE:	DATE:
1. Aim What were you aiming to do?	
2. Introduction a) Did the introduction set the scene for the aim? b) Did it cause you to want to listen to the rest of the sermon?	
3. Structure a) What were the main points? b) Did you give yourself as well as information?	
4. Text a) Was the text properly understood and explained? b) Was it set in its immediate context? c) Was it set in its biblical context?	
5. Illustrations a) Were they clear and did they illustrate the point being made? b) Were they well-spaced?	
6. Voice Was there variation in the pace and volume?	
7. What was the best feature of the talk?	
8. Where would you improve it?	
9. What action did you take as a result of this talk?	

About Matthias Media

Ever since 'St Matthias Press and Tapes' first opened its doors in 1988, under the auspices of St Matthias Anglican Church, Centennial Park, in Sydney, our aim has been to provide the Christian community with products of a uniformly high standard— both in their biblical faithfulness and in the quality of the writing and production.

Now known as Matthias Media, we have grown to become an international provider of user-friendly resources for ministry, with Christians of all sorts using our Bible studies, books, Briefings, audio cassettes, videos, training courses—you name it.

For more information about the range of Matthias Media resources, call us on Freecall **1800 814 360** (or in Sydney 9663-1478), or fax us on (02) 9662-4289, and we will send you a free catalogue. Or you can e-mail us at <**sales@matthiasmedia.com.au**>. Or visit our Web site at: **http://www.matthiasmedia.com.au**

A Fresh Start

by John Chapman

Something is terribly wrong—
with our world, with our
relationships, with us. We all
sense this at different times.
But is there anything that can
be done about it?

With all the honesty and
humour for which he is famous,
John Chapman tells us in
A Fresh Start that God has
done something about it.
We read about:

- just what God has done for us through his Son, Jesus;
- how we can know it is true;
- what the alternatives are;
- and what we should do about it.

If you have been searching for a book that simply and clearly
explains what it means to be a Christian, either for your own or
another's benefit, your search is over.

ANOTHER RESOURCE FOR GROWING CHRISTIANS
FROM MATTHIAS MEDIA

**Look for these title in your local Christian bookstore,
or order direct from Matthias Media.**

Know and Tell the Gospel

by John Chapman

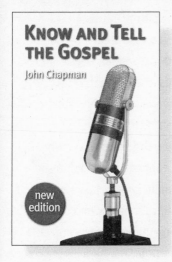

Know and Tell the Gospel deals with all the questions that so quickly come to mind when we think about sharing our faith. Just what is the gospel anyway? Is it my job to explain it to people? What is God's role and what is mine? Where does church fit in? Why is evangelism so often hard? And how can we train ourselves and others to be involved?

In his characteristically friendly and engaging way, 'Chappo' provides warm encouragement, insightful biblical teaching, and a wealth of practical information on evangelism for all Christians. This new edition has been extensively revised and re-written, and contains up-to-date information and evaluation on current resources for evangelism.

Look for these title in your local Christian bookstore, or order direct from Matthias Media.

Giving the Talk Video

by John Chapman

GIVING
THE
talk

CHAPPO ON PREACHING

a training video
on biblical preaching
featuring
John Chapman

Imagine sitting at the feet of one of the greatest preachers Australia has known, and learning from his 50 years of experience in giving Christian talks. That's what is on offer in this training video, featuring the wit and wisdom of John Chapman. 'Chappo', as he is universally known, has a wealth of experience not only in preaching, but in teaching others to preach. In *Giving the Talk* he passes on the basics of preparing and delivering biblical sermons, the traps to avoid, the great benefits of success.

Whether you're a novice speaker, or a hardened veteran, there's plenty in Chappo's presentation to inform, provoke and inspire.

Look for these title in your local Christian bookstore, or order direct from Matthias Media.

ANOTHER RESOURCE FOR GR... FROM MATTHIAS MEDIA

Bible Teaching on Tape

Matthias Media also has an extensive range of reorded sermons—including many excellent examples of evangelistic talks by evangelists such as Phillip Jensen, John Chapman and Alan Stewart.

Our complete electronic tape catalogue can be found by following the link from our main Web page (www.matthiasmedia.com.au) and is available in both Filemaker Pro (version 3) and DBF formats. You can open and search the DBF format using most Database or Spreadsheet applications.

Choose from over 1,700 tapes.

You can use tapes...
- to learn from experienced and gifted speakers
- to supplement the teaching you receive at Church
- to help you prepare for leading a study or giving a talk
- to give away to non-Christians to explain the Gospel
- to lend or give away to fellow Christians to help them sort through an issue
- to bring to life some of that 'dead' time like driving or ironing

Order direct from Matthias Media
Email: tapes@matthiasmedia.com.au